EQUITY COMPENSATION FOR LIMITED LIABILITY COMPANIES

EQUITY COMPENSATION FOR LIMITED LIABILITY COMPANIES

Brian Hector • Daniel Janich • Alan Nadel • Corey Rosen

The National Center for Employee Ownership
Oakland, California

Equity Compensation for Limited Liability Companies
Book design by Scott S. Rodrick

The National Center for Employee Ownership
1736 Franklin Street, 8th Floor
Oakland, CA 94612
(510) 208-1300
(510) 272-9510 (fax)
Web site: www.nceo.org

ISBN: 1-932924-61-2
ISBN-13: 978-1-932924-61-9

Contents

Preface

Corey Rosen

Executive Director, National Center for Employee Ownership (NCEO)

For many years, the most common advice on sharing equity with employees in a limited liability company (LLC) has been "switch to S corporation status instead." The argument was that it was too complicated to share equity in an LLC. Yet many LLC company leaders want to share equity with employees and have very good reasons for retaining their company's status as an LLC. When I asked experts in employee ownership law if it were possible to share equity in an LLC, the usual response was "yes, but it is complicated." No one seemed to want to go into too much detail about just what these complications were, however.

So after many years of telling people that, yes, it is possible, but that we did not have any specific material or advice on the topic (because we could not find anyone who had written about it in more than the most general terms), we decided to create our own material. This book is the product of that effort. It is, we believe, the only detailed exploration of equity compensation in limited liability companies available.

The book starts with my general description of LLCs and an overview of the ways to share equity. In chapter 2, I explore alternative approaches to designing plans in terms of who gets what, how much they get, when they get it, and what triggers the awards. In chapter 3, Daniel Janich, an attorney in this field and NCEO board member, and I provide more detail on the specific ways to share equity in an LLC, with a particular focus on tax issues. In chapter 4, Alan Nadel, one of the leading national experts on accounting for equity compensation plans, describes how these plans affect a company's financial statements. In chapter 5, I describe the various kinds of equity sharing methods available in S or C corporations. The idea here is to let readers judge whether the somewhat broader range of choices for such corporations justifies switching from LLC status. In the appendix, Brian Hector, an attorney specializing in all forms of employee ownership and a frequent speaker at NCEO meetings, provides a model LLC equity compensation plan. A CD-ROM with the plan document in two word-processing formats (Microsoft Word and Rich Text Format) is bound into the back of the book.

Daniel, Alan, and Brian all have also provided very useful input on the chapters I wrote, as well as for the general concepts of the book. There could not have been a book without their help; indeed, they are among the few people we have found nationally who have the kind of detailed knowledge of this issue that could make this book possible. Their efforts are greatly appreciated.

CHAPTER 1

A Primer on Limited Liability Companies

Corey Rosen

Limited liability companies (LLCs) have become a very popular way to organize new and smaller enterprises. They offer the advantages of partnership taxation treatment (although a choice can be made to be taxed as a corporation), limited personal liability for the owners, flexibility in the distribution of earnings, flatter governance and management structure, and fewer paperwork requirements than S or C corporations. On the other hand, they do require that owners pay income taxes on their share of company earnings even if not distributed, often are not attractive to venture capital and private equity investors, and face differing laws in various states. Furthermore, the LLC structure is more cumbersome and a less efficient vehicle for offering equity compensation to employees than S or C corporations are.

LLC owners often say that they formed their company as an LLC because their attorney or advisor said they should. While some people clearly think through the pros and cons of different legal forms for conducting their business, others just take this advice without questioning whether an LLC really is the best choice. This book provides a basic overview of LLC issues. Because state laws for LLCs vary, and tax and other requirements can vary even more, it is important for business owners to work closely with their advisors to make sure they understand all the implications of choosing the LLC form of business. No one publication can provide the kind of detailed advice applicable to every situation.

What Is an LLC?

The limited liability company is a relatively new type of business form. Wyoming passed the first LLC law in 1977; the other states eventually followed suit. While the laws for LLCs are similar from one jurisdiction to another and sometimes identical, they are not all the same. Some states impose entity taxes on LLCs; a few impose some level of income tax. A few states have different governance requirements as well. If an LLC operates in more than one state, it may be subject to multiple tax and possibly governance rules.

The impetus behind the creation of LLC law was to provide a more simple and flexible way for small businesses to organize than corporate law usually permits. It was intended that businesses would be taxed as proprietorships or partnerships while providing their owners with the limited liability available to corporate shareholders. LLCs are owned by "members" rather than shareholders. The term is roughly analogous to partners or shareholders, but with some notable differences. LLCs must have at least two members if they are to be taxed as partnerships (a one-owner LLC will be taxed as a sole proprietorship or a corporation for federal tax purposes). The members create an "operating agreement" that functions similarly to a corporation's bylaws. The agreement specifies how the LLC will be governed and managed, how profits and losses will be allocated, and member rights (including voting, buy-sell arrangements, and distributions of earnings). LLC agreements can specify whether a member will be the manager or someone else will serve in that capacity.

Key Organizational Issues

Limited Liability

Like corporate shareholders, LLC members can avoid personal responsibility for losses or liabilities of the LLC beyond what the LLC can pay. This is not an unlimited right, however. Several circumstances can still "pierce the corporate veil" and give rise to personal liability, including:

- Contracts that members sign, such as personal guarantees for debt or performance
- Failure to deposit taxes withheld from employee wages
- Intentional fraud, reckless behavior, or illegal acts
- Personal and direct injury of someone or property

In some cases, the "corporate veil" may also be pierced if tax authorities can sustain the position that the LLC is really not an entity separate from a member's personal interests. Establishing one's house as an LLC to avoid personal liability for defaulting on the underlying mortgage, for instance, would not be effective protection.

Governance

Unlike a corporation, an LLC does not require a board of directors, although some kind of governing or advisory body may be advisable, and may be required if there are outside investors. Instead, an LLC's members make decisions about the company subject to the operating agreement. A few states require more formal governance procedures, however, such as an annual member meeting, something normally only required of a corporation.

Allocation of Earnings

Unlike S or C corporations, LLCs need not allocate earnings pro rata to capital ownership. In an S corporation, owners receive a share of earnings based on their respective percentages of corporate ownership; in C corporations, distributions of earnings are based on specified stock rights but must be proportional to ownership within the same classes of stock. LLC members are taxed not necessarily based on their membership interest percentage, but rather based on whatever agreement the members have made for allocating earnings. This agreement may be stated in the operating agreement, may take the form of income-only partnership interests, or may be just an understanding among the LLC members.

Another difference between a corporation and an LLC is the manner and extent to which the business's earnings are allocated annually. In the case of an LLC, all of the net income of the business is allocable to the members who pay personal income tax on their respective amounts regardless of distributions they receive during the applicable year. Similarly to partners in a partnership, the LLC members may agree that a partner may be allocated a disproportionate percentage of the LLC earnings based on whatever business factors they choose.

This flexibility is one of the major advantages of an LLC. It is especially useful in the case of LLCs where one party invests capital (e.g., venture capital or private equity) and another puts in "sweat equity" (i.e., performance of services for less than full pay). In an S corporation, for instance, if a shareholder purchases 20% of the corporate stock, then he or she will be allocated 20% of the corporate net earnings. But if that same 20% shareholder purchases 20% of the stock and also puts in a year of sweat equity to build the business, he or she may not receive more than a 20% share of the corporate net income, although the parties could agree to also pay additional compensation in recognition of the shareholder's efforts. In the same situation with an LLC, however, the LLC members may simply choose to allocate a greater portion of the company's net earnings to that individual to compensate for sweat equity. Alternatively, they may agree to compensate the individual by awarding more ownership (i.e., member units) in the LLC.

The allocation-of-earnings approach must have a substantial economic effect; i.e., there must be a good business reason for doing it, other than to avoid taxation. Provided the allocation of earnings is not based on tax avoidance, the allocation generally will be respected by the IRS. Allocating more earnings to an owner with a lower tax rate and less to one with a higher rate, absent some other compelling business reason, likely would be problematic. Similarly, care should be taken with the allocation of passive income and losses in an LLC, a subject beyond the scope of this primer. This should be discussed with a tax professional prior to making any special allocations of income or loss.

Members

S corporations are permitted to have up to 100 shareholders and still retain the S corporation status. In contrast, LLCs and C corporations may have an unlimited number of members or shareholders. S corporations may have only one class of stock; LLCs and C corporations can have different rights attributed to different classes of ownership. S corporations may not be owned by certain prohibited entities, including C corporations, other S corporations, most non-taxable entities, most trusts, other LLCs, partnerships, or nonresident aliens. LLCs may be owned by anyone. LLCs are rarely used in some industries (e.g., venture capital) because the associated tax effects are inconsistent with the objectives of the owners. LLC members also may have different rights or benefits attached to their ownership besides how earnings are allocated, such as special distributions, governance, or the ability to cash out their ownership interests.

Dissolution

The LLC has a permanent life unless a time of dissolution is specified in the operating agreement. Similarly, one or more members may leave and the other members agree to continue the business. The operating agreement must be specific on this eventuality to avoid inadvertent termination.

Mergers and Other Ownership Transfers

If an LLC is merged into another company, it is not eligible for tax-free reorganization as provided by Internal Revenue Code Section 368. The LLC can first be terminated and S or C status chosen, but if the change and merger come within a close time frame, it will likely be considered a "step transaction," whereby the IRS takes the position that it is still an LLC.

LLCs can, however, be sold to other companies just like corporations, subject to the tax issues discussed below. Ownership interests can also be transferred to anyone or any entity, with some restrictions varying by state. In S corporations, by contrast, transfers can be made only to other S owners.

Taxes

A limited liability company is taxed as a sole proprietorship (if there is only one owner) or a partnership unless the LLC "checks the box" on an IRS filing to be taxed as a corporation. As a sole proprietorship or partnership, members are taxed on their pro-rata share of earnings unless the operating agreement specifies otherwise. This is the share of the actual earnings of the LLC, not the earnings that are distributed (earnings may be retained to grow the company, for instance). These earnings, in turn, are taxed at the individual member's personal tax rates. Members usually must make quarterly estimated income tax payments. While the federal government levies no tax on the LLC, some states do.

One difference between an LLC and an S corporation or C corporation is the manner in which earnings are subject to payroll taxes. In a corporation, when a shareholder-employee receives compensation, the employee pays half of the payroll taxes (through withholding) and the company pays the other half. In an LLC, the member pays the full amount of the payroll taxes in the form of self-employment tax. The total is currently 12.4% of pay up to the current year's Social Security wage base for the Social Security component of self-employment tax, plus 2.9% of all pay for the Medicare component. Although the LLC member pays twice what an S corporation shareholder pays, they both pay the same when the S corporation's share of taxes is also considered.

Another difference between a corporation and an LLC is the manner and extent to which the business's earnings are taxed each year. In the case of an LLC, all of the net income of the business is allocable to the members who pay personal income tax on their allocated amounts regardless of distributions they receive during the applicable year. If a member has a 40% interest in an LLC and the LLC earns a profit of $100,000 during the year, that member is allocated $40,000 of income even if he or she receives only a $20,000 distribution. On the other hand, a C corporation that earns a profit of $100,000 must pay corporate income tax on the full amount. If a distribution of that income (e.g., a dividend) is made to shareholders, they must pay income tax on those distributed amounts. Hence, the use of a C corporation usually results in double taxation of the corporate profits.

At the time of sale of LLC member units, a single capital gains tax generally is imposed on the gain (with some exceptions, e.g., receivables). This is different from a C (but not S) corporation, where an *asset* sale would trigger double taxation by virtue of a corporate capital gains tax on the appreciated value of the assets for the corporation and another capital gains tax for the shareholders on the sale of the company's shares. A *stock* sale, however, generally is not subject to double taxation, and a merger for stock in the acquirer may be tax-deferred altogether.

Conclusion

The flexibility of LLCs makes them attractive vehicles for those who wish for the flexibility of a proprietorship or partnership while retaining legal protection for the owners. Unfortunately, while they are simpler and more flexible than C or S corporations, they are considerably less so on issues concerning equity compensation for employees. In fact, some advisors suggest that companies wishing to share equity with employees should select regular corporate status because employees more readily understand stock options and restricted stock than partnership interests. We believe they may be too hasty in their recommendations, as the rest of this book will show. Equity compensation in the case of an LLC can provide for significant incentives that are performance-based. The range of choices may be narrower in the case of an LLC, and there are some remaining tax uncertainties and complexities, but effective performance-based incentives certainly can be structured in the LLC.

Chapter 2

Designing an Equity Incentive Plan

Corey Rosen

A variety of issues must be considered when designing an equity compensation plan for employees in an LLC. This chapter is not intended to provide specific guidelines on how to structure a plan but rather to raise the issues companies need to consider. In making these decisions, company leaders should consult with peers and advisors as well as evaluate available survey data on industry practices.

How Much to Share

The first decision is how much ownership to share. The most typical way owners of closely held companies decide how much ownership to share is by setting aside an amount of equity or equity rights that is within the maximum dilution level with which they are comfortable. This approach can create problems, however.

Typically, once this number is set, a large portion of this equity is either provided immediately to existing employees or allocated to employees over a few years. The problem with this strategy is that allocating too much too quickly leaves relatively little equity to give to new employees. In a growing company, that can lead to a severe problem in attracting and retaining good people. It can also create two classes of employees, some with large equity grants and some without them. Moreover, this model often does not create an explicit link between employee effort and the rewards of ownership.

A second approach focuses on what percentage of compensation must be provided in the form of equity in order to attract, retain, and motivate people. These decisions need to be based on competitive considerations of what people could receive elsewhere as well as on discussions with employees to get a sense of how much they expect. Finding relevant information about competitive pay practices means more than simply referring to a salary survey. Competitive pay information should be based on data from companies that might compete for the same employees, rather than just the company's business competitors. Often this includes companies in other industries that may hire individuals with similar experiences and skill sets as those of the company's current employees.

Rather than thinking about "how much" in terms of a total percentage of company shares or total compensation, it might make sense to use a more dynamic model based on performance. In this approach, the issue for existing owners is not "what percentage of the company do we own?" but "how much is what we own worth?" Owners in this model would rather own 10% of a $11 million company than 90% of a $1 million company. This notion can be incorporated into an explicit plan by telling employees that if the company meets or exceeds certain targets, they will receive a percentage of the incremental value created by that performance in the form of equity or equity rights. If the company exceeds its goals, then, by definition, sharing part of the surplus value leaves both the employees and the existing owners better off than they would have been. The targets can be based on whatever performance goals are appropriate for the company, such as sales, profits, market penetration, or whatever else is critical to the company's future. In the current economic environment, the company should also include risk management considerations in the selection of relevant performance targets.

It is also important to consider the "internal equity" of awards. A common problem in equity plans is that employees believe they are not getting what they deserve, something they assess primarily based on what they perceive other people are receiving. Few employees would argue that everyone should be paid the same, but most would contend that everyone should receive awards consistent with their relative contributions to the company. This problem has been starkest in relationship to executive pay, but even at rank-and-file levels, it is not uncommon for companies to pay people doing very similar jobs very different amounts of equity, perhaps because of the timing of when they came to work (more awards were available or the shares were more opportunely priced) or what was perceived as necessary to hire them. Nobel Prize-winning research has shown that perceived equity in economic transactions will often trump purely "rational" economic logic. Employees will be more cynical and demotivated if they believe that their awards are inequitable relative to what top executives receive. Boards and compensation consultants may (rightly or wrongly) argue that this can benefit the entire company, but employees will be slower to accept these arguments than the CEO's peers.

What Kind of Equity?

The kinds of equity vehicles a company chooses depend largely on the purposes of the plan. While that may seem obvious, it is far too common for companies to select an equity vehicle because "that's what other people do," or "that's what my advisor understood best," or "I didn't know there were other ways to do it." Beware of advisors whose discouragement of one kind of a plan or another may really be their way of saying, "I don't know how to do the other types."

Sharing equity in LLCs is more challenging than in S or C corporations. In fact, as noted in the preface to this book, advisors frequently tell clients that if they want to share equity with employees, they should switch to S corporation status, which allows them to use options, phantom stock, restricted stock, stock appreciation rights, and similar plans. S corporations are taxed similarly to LLCs, but are less flexible in terms of how earnings are distributed. While employee equity awards in LLCs present more complex tax considerations than is the case in S or C corporations, there are approaches that can be effective.

Forms of Equity Available in an LLC

There are two main forms of equity interests available in an LLC:

- *Capital interests:* Capital interests can be compared to restricted stock in an S or C corporation. They grant the employee the right to share in the capital value of the company through the receipt of a share of the proceeds upon sale of the company.

- *Profits interests:* A profits interest will entitle the owner both to capital appreciation and profits of the business.

Either type of interest may be subject to restrictions, such as a vesting requirement. Either may be forfeited if the employee is engaged in wrongdoing at the company or goes to work for a competitor. Companies can also issue an option to acquire these interests at a later point based on a current price.

Alternatively, the company can use equity equivalent rights (also called "virtual options," "unit appreciation rights," and other names that help explain the concept), which are equivalent to stock appreciation rights in an S or C corporation. The company gives the employees a grant of a hypothetical number of capital interest or profit interest units. On vesting, any increase in the value of these units is paid in cash, much as a bonus would be paid. The right could also be structured so that the employee received the entire value of a capital or profits interest, somewhat like the grant of phantom shares in an S or C corporation. In this discussion, we will call awards that grant an increase in value equity appreciation rights and ones that provide the full value phantom equity (terminology parallel to the concepts of stock appreciation rights and phantom stock in C or S corporations).

Another form of compensation that is common to many LLCs (particularly private equity and hedge funds) is the "carried interest," a perceived form of equity. Essentially, a carried interest is the right to share in the profits of the LLC. In partnership terminology, this is called a "profits interest." If structured properly, a carried interest entitles the employee to a predetermined portion of the LLC's profits, calculated after all expenses have been paid. In some cases it is based on the net income of the LLC, whereas in others it is a modification of net income (e.g., EBITDA or a variation thereof). Although the carried interest is not actually equity in the LLC, it can be designed in a manner that provides the holder with an ongoing right to future income and that can be sold or otherwise transferred to others, depending on its terms and the operating agreement of the LLC.

Basic Tax Issues

An employee's receipt of a profits interest (including a carried interest) in exchange for services is not taxable upon grant if certain safe harbor tax requirements are satisfied, including the requirement that the interest not be sold within two years of receipt. If these requirements are not satisfied, there is some uncertainty about the income tax consequences arising from the grant of a profits interest to an employee. When the employee redeems his or her profits interest (by selling it back to the company or to a third party), the gain is taxed as either a short-term or long-term capital gain, depending upon how long the interest was held by the employee. It should be noted that some tax advisors have expressed concern about whether capital gain treatment is available for employees who initially received a profits interest for no cost, while other advisors do not share that concern. Employees with profits interests are taxed as partners rather than as employees, so their income is reported on a Schedule K-1 and is not subject to income tax withholding.

An employee who receives a capital interest in exchange for services recognizes compensation income in the year of the award. The amount of income that is recognized equals the fair market value of the interest at the time of grant, less anything paid by the employee for the capital interest. If the interest is subject to a substantial risk of forfeiture and is nontransferable, as is typically the case, then the recognition of ordinary income tax is delayed until the forfeiture restriction lapses, unless the employee makes a timely Section 83(b) election. If a Section 83(b) election is not made, then ordinary income tax is paid on the value of the award at the time it vests. Any additional appreciation in the value of the capital interest is subject to either long- or short-term capital gain tax, depending upon how long the capital interest is held following recognition of ordinary income.

If a Section 83(b) election is made but the award never vests, the employee may not claim a refund from the IRS for the ordinary income taxes that were paid. The company receives a tax deduction for any amounts on which the employee pays ordinary income tax. Under the partnership taxation rules, there is a question about whether there is also a "deemed sale" when a capital interest is awarded or forfeited, resulting in potential income tax consequences for other holders of capital interests in the company.

Granting an option to acquire either a capital interest or profits interest is not a taxable event for either the employee or the company. The exercise of an option on a capital interest will result in taxable income for the employee and a deduction for the company. The exercise of an option on a profits interest would not be taxable for the employee or deductible for the company if the tax requirements for nonrecognition of tax on a profits interest were satisfied.

For tax purposes, equity appreciation rights are treated in the same way as a bonus: the employee pays ordinary income tax on the receipt of the cash award, and the company is entitled to a corresponding tax deduction.

Complexity Concerns

Many companies will choose one kind of award or another because it is less complex to administer, understand, and tax. This is more of an issue in an LLC, where the tax issues can be very complex and somewhat uncertain. In fact, this is why many advisors urge companies to switch to S status, where the tax issues are simpler. If employees find they have a great deal of difficulty understanding how an award works, or see the tax treatment as just too difficult to grasp relative to other kinds of pay, the value of the award can be diminished substantially. It might be better to choose a simpler alternative equity approach, such as equity equivalent awards, even if these awards may have less favorable long-term tax consequences because they never qualify for capital gain treatment.

As with all the choices below, keep in mind that companies can give different employees different kinds or mixes of awards, with different rules being applicable to each.

Granting Existing Value or the Value of Future Increases Only

Capital interests, profits interests, or phantom equity give the employee the existing value of the ownership plus any appreciation (much like giving an employee a share with or without dividend rights in a corporation). That means the employee reaps the benefit of the embedded value that has been previously created. This would be most logical in cases where the company has been running for a while, and the early employees have not yet received any equity awards. "Full-value" awards effectively give these employees some retroactive benefit for their work. These awards also make sense if the intention is to ensure that employees receive something even if the value of the company does not increase or increases too slowly to make the awards appealing.

In contrast, options on a capital interest or profits interest, like equity appreciation rights, provide only a share in the future growth in value. If a company is granting awards very early on when there is little existing value, these appreciation-based awards can provide significant value to employees, much like full-value awards. Down the road, however, they are very different.

One problem with appreciation-based awards is that the single most important factor in determining their value is volatility. In the formula that accountants use to assess the present value of the award of a stock option, for instance, volatility is the single most important factor. This may seem counterintuitive. Wouldn't you prefer an option on a stock that has less dramatic ups and downs? But consider that with an option, you can ignore the downs (just don't exercise the options) and take advantage of the ups. A more stable stock has lower high points (but also higher low points), providing less of this leveraging opportunity.

This has a number of additional insidious effects. First, it can encourage excessive risk-taking by top decision-makers, especially if their expected time horizon with the company is shorter than the term of the equity award. Second, it introduces a lottery effect into the incentive structure. Two employees receiving identical awards may have significantly different opportunities for gains if they were hired at different dates when the equity had a different value. Finally, appreciation-based awards can engender cynicism among employees who view equity as a lottery whose benefits may go to the lucky and to the insiders who know best when to exercise.

This may be less of an issue in an LLC than it is in other companies, especially public companies. LLC valuations tend to be done annually, absent some specific event, and may "smooth out" some of the external factors that create volatility for stocks in general. Nonetheless, LLCs can still be subject to the same problems as corporations, especially if the market for their products or services is highly variable.

Who Is Eligible and Who Will Actually Get Equity?

In the past, the answer to the question of who was eligible was very simple for most companies: just the "key" people. In some ways, this is still how companies view equity; it is just that their definition of "key" has changed. For many companies, everyone is a key person. Many LLC companies have a flat management structure and are pushing down more decision-making to all levels, asking employees to make business decisions on a regular basis. Managers at these companies reason that if they want people to think and act like owners, they should make them owners. At the same time, for some companies in some labor markets, it is necessary to provide options at all levels just to attract and retain people. For companies in these situations, the answer to "who's eligible?" is simple—everyone is.

One set of issues that some companies consider, but that they probably should not, is the so-called "1/n" or "free rider" effect, and the related "line-of-sight" problem. The argument here is that an equity award cannot be much of an incentive to an employee who cannot see (has no line of sight to) just how his or her work actually affects the value of the business. This is especially problematic in larger organizations where employees not only don't have a clear line of sight to the award but also can figure they can "free ride" on the efforts of others.

These arguments are appealing but empirically wrong. Research shows that motivation at work is much more complicated than a simple economic calculation. Few employees go to work each day thinking, "If I do x, I get y, but if I do x + a, I get y + b, so if y + b is large enough, I'll do x + a." In reality, this is really not the case. Research shows again and again that most people's efforts at work are a function of how well their job functions fit their skills, whether they have opportunities for meaningful input into decisions affecting their jobs, how much they trust management and management trusts them, whether they find the job engaging, and whether they believe what they and the company do has value.

Equity sharing becomes important in this context not so much as an incentive for behavior but as a reward. If people are asked to act like owners and are treated like owners, they will be more productive and make larger contributions in terms of new ideas and information. If they then are denied an opportunity to benefit from what they add, they will feel manipulated and back away. If, on the other hand, they feel they are equitably rewarded relative to what others contribute or that they are all part of a team sharing in the results, they are much more likely to stay committed. So the question of who gets equity should be based on which employees should be thinking and acting like owners.

Tenure

At the simplest level, companies can require that people work a minimum amount of time, often one year, before they become eligible for equity awards. This ensures that each employee has at least some commitment to the company.

Full-Time/Part-Time

In the past, it was unusual to provide equity to part-time employees. Innovators like Southwest Airlines, however, have provided options to everyone, arguing that many of their part-time people would (or if properly rewarded could) become long-term employees.

Performance or a Universal Rule?

Equity can be granted according to some kind of merit judgment; on a regular, universal schedule such as annually, or upon hiring or promotion; or it can be granted or vest upon the achievement of individual, group, or corporate objectives. These methods are not mutually exclusive; many companies use a combination of these techniques.

The core issue here is that, on the one hand, including everyone who is eligible according to some formula rules out management discretion, which employees may see as arbitrary or political. It also may help foster a team atmosphere in which everyone sees that they have a stake. On the other hand, some employees may feel cheated if they think they have been exceptional performers but receive unexceptional rewards. This suggests that some combination of the two can be appealing, provided the basis for rewarding excellence is one that most or all employees see as reasonably fair—a tricky business, but one many companies have done well at, albeit in a variety of ways. Some companies, for instance, use 360-degree performance reviews in which everyone reviews everyone else, others use very specific and transparent financial or other measurable targets, and others seek employee input in designing rating systems.

A typical merit-based approach would provide work unit managers (or a single manager in a smaller company) with a number of awards that can be granted to employees in the group based on performance appraisals. An alternative to individual merit judgments is to provide that a pool of equity awards will be given to a work team upon the achievement of the team's goals. Many companies, of course, will simply name specific individuals, usually top managers, who will receive equity, but the company will define their allocation based on merit assessments of some sort.

At the other end of the spectrum is an automatic formula based on salary levels. This can be for one employee or every employee. For instance, a number of larger companies provide all employees who meet basic service requirements with 10% of pay every year in stock options. The argument behind such formulas is that salary reflects management's judgment of an employee's contributions to the company, and equity is simply another form of compensation.

Many companies provide awards on hiring, then make additional grants periodically or upon promotion. Linking additional grants to promotion gives employees an incentive to improve their skills and rewards those people the organization believes are making greater contributions. On the other hand, an overemphasis on promotion-related grants can mean that employees who are very good performers but who are not in jobs that can easily lead to a promotion are overlooked.

Refresher grants give employees additional awards when they exercise some of the options or other equity benefits they were previously granted. For instance, if an employee has 1,000 options on a capital or profits interest and exercises 200, then the employee would be given new options on another 200 shares at exercise. The theory here is to maintain a constant level of ownership interest in the company. Similarly, refresher awards might be granted when the company issues additional equity interests so that an employee maintains the same percentage of potential ownership as was held before the dilution. While these automatic additional grants help to keep the employee's equity interest high, other owners might object to the ongoing dilution.

How Often Should Awards Be Granted?

Equity inherently involves risk, but the design of plans can accentuate that risk. Companies that provide one-time grants of appreciation-based awards and grant them only upon an event, such as hiring, promotion, or meeting some corporate target, wind up with employees whose ownership interest in the company is based on the price of stock at a single point in time. This is not a problem with full-value awards, which do not have an exercise price based on the stock's trading price on the grant date.

Granting appreciation-based awards infrequently accelerates the risk of equity both for the employee and the company because equity granted at a high price may never be "in the money"; awards granted at a low price may cost the company more than it ever intended when the awards are redeemed. Employees who happen to receive their equity awards at a good time end up doing very well, while those who receive their grants when the price is not so favorable don't do well at all. Creating an ownership culture of "we're all in this together" can be very difficult in these circumstances.

For many companies, the best way to deal with these potential problems is to provide grants in smaller amounts but more frequently or to grant full-value awards such as restricted equity or phantom equity. Frequent grants work best for companies using equity as a compensation strategy. Startups whose equity value is close to zero or that use large initial grants to attract people away from other opportunities may find this less appropriate. It also is not appropriate for companies that want simply to make occasional grants at the discretion of the company, often on the attainment of some corporate milestone. These companies see equity more as a symbolic reward than as ongoing ownership strategy.

The periodic allocation "dollar-cost averages" the awards, smoothing bumps in volatile markets. This approach also gives employees more of a long-term, ongoing stake in the company. With the vesting schedules attached to the repeated grants of awards, employees are provided an even longer-term interest in the company's performance. Finally, there will be fewer big winners and losers among employees with otherwise similar jobs.

Frequent grants are not all good news, of course. The more often awards are granted, the more complex their administration becomes. There is much more data entry, many more forms to file and disseminate, and many more errors that can be made. It may also become complicated because of frequent tax withholding and tax reporting.

When Will Employees Be Able to Use the Awards?

There are two principal issues in deciding when employees will be able to translate their equity into cash: vesting and exercise periods. Vesting generally provides that an employee accrues an increasing right to the awards granted based on the number of years worked. However, there is a growing use of performance vesting, in which vesting is a function of company, group, or individual performance. As various targets are met, the equity awards become increasingly vested. The exercise period is the time between an award's vesting and its expiration. Some types of awards may vest automatically upon exercise, especially equity-equivalent rights. Outright grants of capital or profits interests might vest at grant, but more commonly would have a vesting period. Once vested, there typically would be no further deferral of the actual receipt of the award.

Options present a different scenario. Here the employee might become fully vested in a right to acquire a profits or capital interest, but choose to defer it until later for tax or cash flow reasons. The most common exercise period for stock options in S or C corporations is ten years. Grants of restricted stock (stock that is tradable only after certain conditions, such as working for a defined period of time, are met) do not have an exercise period; instead, the restrictions lapse upon vesting, typically after three to five years. Given that many LLCs may have shorter time horizons than public companies (they may be working toward a sale or an initial public offering), they may want a shorter period in which an award can be exercised.

Vesting schedules are fairly consistent across companies, with three- to five-year graduated vesting the most common schedule. Sales, profit targets, and cash flow are the most common performance triggers. A few companies allow employees to exercise their awards only when a defined event occurs, such as the achievement of a certain stock price or earnings goal. This accomplishes two things. First, it provides an incentive to meet the goal, and second, it reassures investors that dilution will occur only if the company meets certain targets. Once these targets are met, employees are normally given a certain amount of time to exercise the award, anywhere from a few months to several years. Alternatively, a company could provide that awards can be exercised only upon the occurrence of an event, such as a sale or going public.

In closely held companies, allowing exercise of an award only upon sale of the company or an IPO is a very common approach. If an option is exercised or the company allows restricted stock to vest before then, employees end up owning stock and having a tax obligation. Unless the company can provide a market for the shares (an issue discussed below), this combination may not be perceived by the employee as much of a reward. Companies and employees must evaluate just how likely these events are to occur, however. Management is often excessively optimistic about how marketable the company is.

It is also important to consider that if equity compensation awards all become exercisable upon sale or an IPO, buyers of the stock may not find the company so valuable. A growing number of closely held companies are restricting exercise to sometime after a sale or an IPO (in a sale situation, this requires the acquiring company to provide options in the new employer) to ensure that there are adequate employee incentives in place following the sale or IPO.

Providing a Market for the Shares

Providing for liquidity of equity awards is one of the most important of all design issues. Most closely held companies solve the problem by limiting the exercise or sale of equity awards to when the company is sold or goes public. This makes sense for companies that realistically see these alternatives as likely to happen in the foreseeable future. Some company leaders, however, assume that they can provide for marketability only upon these events because a closely held company, for one reason or another, cannot provide a market itself. There are, in fact, alternatives for those companies and for companies that prefer to stay closely held and have no plans to sell or become public. These companies can provide an internal market by buying back the equity interests themselves or allowing other employees to buy them. This requires proper cash flow planning. Alternatively, an LLC could convert to a C or S corporation and set up an employee stock ownership plan (ESOP), which can buy the equity (now converted into shares) with pretax dollars through an ESOP trust.

Purchasing vs. Grant

A key consideration for many employers is whether employees should pay anything for their equity. At one extreme are employers in closely held companies who see the chance to own equity as itself a valuable benefit, even if it is offered at fair market value. At the other are those who believe employees cannot or should not take the risk to invest in company equity, but do want them to have a stake in the company. Several considerations apply to any choice on this matter:

- Do employees have the resources to buy equity? If not, is the company willing to lend them the money? If the loan carries an interest rate less than fair market value, there are possible tax implications with respect to the loan.

- How many employees will buy equity, either at full value or a discount? The results are often surprising and disappointing and may not provide enough people with an equity stake to accomplish the "ownership culture" objectives the company hopes to achieve.

- Even if many employees buy equity, will the distribution of ownership be enough to create a real stake in the outcome for most people? Employees whose financial obligations (or consumer preferences) leave them with little discretionary income, as well as employees who are risk-averse, may end up with only token amounts of equity.

- If there is a discount, how much will it be? Discounts may result in taxable income to the employee.

- Where options are issued, is paying for the exercise of an option good enough? If an employee uses cash or shares to exercise an option, is that enough to satisfy the company's desire to have people buy shares, even though there is a certain gain for those who sell their shares immediately?

In most companies, widespread ownership does not occur solely through an equity purchase plan. For some companies, however, broad ownership is not the goal. Rather, the objective is to engage specific employees and/or to raise capital. There is a perception that executives will have a greater interest in the company's success if they have some "skin in the game."

Perceptions vs. Reality

In classical economics, people are "rational" economic actors by definition. That means that they make choices about things based on maximizing their economic value. For instance, if people have the choice of having $1,000 now or a guaranteed $1,200 12 months from now, as rational actors, they would wait. It turns out that in reality this is not an accurate model of how people behave. Three notable characteristics are especially important for equity awards:

- People overvalue current rewards: Most people in the example above take the $1,000 now. They greatly undervalue the time value of money.

- People value upside risk less than downside risk: Researchers have asked people if they would make a double or nothing bet if they had lost $50. Most said yes. But if they had won $50 rather than losing $50, most said they would turn down a double or nothing bet. In the stock market, this helps explain why people hold on to losing shares too long.

- People are willing to pay for perceived fairness: In an often repeated experiment, people are asked to accept or not accept an offer to split $10 between them and someone else. If the split is $5/$5, everyone is happy, but if it is $7 and $3 or less, most people getting the $3 will say no—even though it means neither party gets anything.

An employee equity award works much the same way. The equity award will pay off only well into the future, carries uncertainty about how or if it will be paid for (because it will have liquidity only upon a sale or IPO), has some immediate tax consequences before the recipient is able to cash it in, and is granted to employees in ways that seem inconsistent with their value. All these factors greatly diminish the value of the award in the employees' eyes. As a result, the employer must dole out more than probably it wishes to provide the incentive effect sought. So while employers often want to design awards that seem most favorable to their liquidity, that reward only very long-term employees (even though most people are not sure when they receive the award if they will stay a long time), have no clear liquidity event, and have tax consequences which the employer does not cover, this "favorable" design may be a waste of equity. Similarly, if equity awards are perceived as unfair, employees who receive what they see as the short end of the stick will feel punished, not rewarded, even though the employer is giving them something extra. The employer will be in a worse position (in terms of employee attitudes) than if they had made no grants at all. Consequently, it is imperative in plan design to remember how people actually behave, not how they "should" behave.

Conclusion

Designing an effective equity plan is a difficult balancing act. There are no perfect approaches. The financial and organizational significance of these plans demands that they be considered at least as carefully as any other major investment of company assets and time, not just picked at random or based on limited information. Try to talk to peers who have set up plans (the NCEO can help its members identify other companies with plans), interview different consultants, read enough to feel comfortable with plan structures, and seek the input of board members and, preferably, employees, about what kind of plan will work best—and be prepared to make changes as you learn more.

CHAPTER 3

EQUITY INTERESTS IN LIMITED LIABILITY COMPANIES

Daniel Janich
Corey Rosen

The limited liability company (LLC) is a relatively recent form of business organization available in many, but not all, states that has become increasingly popular. LLCs are similar to corporations in that they provide owners with liability protection but are taxed as partnerships. Because ownership in an LLC is evidenced by membership interests rather than stock, LLCs cannot have employee stock ownership plans (ESOPs), give out stock options, provide restricted stock, or otherwise give employees actual shares or rights to shares. But many LLCs want to reward employees with an equity stake in the company. The proper tax treatment of these equity interests to the recipient and the LLC is not always clear. For this reason, LLCs frequently face formidable challenges in providing employees with an equity interest in the company. This article explores the types of equity interests that an LLC can issue and how such interests are treated for tax purposes.

LLCs in Brief

As in S corporations and partnerships, profits from the operation of an LLC are attributed to the individual owners (referred to as "members"), who pay income tax on them at personal tax rates. Unlike S corporations, however, LLCs, within certain limits, are not required to allocate distributions to members in proportion to their individual ownership interests, provided these "special allocations" have economic substance. IRS rules governing distributions from LLCs are fairly complex, and thus LLC operations generally require guidance from experienced advisors. Although the income taxation of equity interests that are issued by LLCs remains uncertain and complex, with good advice, these challenges should not in themselves be a sufficient reason for a business that is interested in issuing equity incentives to automatically switch to S corporation status.

Advantages and Disadvantages of LLCs vs. S Corporations

When determining whether an LLC should convert to an S corporation, the uncertainties of equity compensation in LLCs should be only one of many considerations to influence the decision.

LLCs have a number of advantages over S corporations besides flexibility in distributions:

- S corporations can have no more than 100 owners; there are no such ownership limits for LLCs.

- Only individuals, certain trusts, and estates can own S corporation stock, but any entity or individual can have an LLC partnership interest, including a non-resident alien.

- LLC members are allocated a tax basis for the debt of the company, meaning losses can be passed through for more than what is invested by a member. The member must actually be liable for the debt repayment, however, if the LLC defaults.

- LLCs can have multiple classes of ownership interests; S corporations can only have one kind of stock. Wholly owned subsidiaries can have their assets, liabilities, and profits treated separately from the LLC.

- LLCs are often used to move assets around in tax-favored ways, such as gifting interests to heirs without providing any attached control rights or moving appreciated property into an LLC without tax consequences. In a corporation, once the assets are taken out, there is a taxable gain.

- LLCs can usually be readily converted to S or C status.

- Some states have entity-level taxes on S corporations but not on LLCs.

- LLCs do not have the same obligations as S or C corporations to keep board minutes or have shareholder resolutions, and they otherwise have fewer compliance burdens than S or C corporations.

- LLCs can provide a profits interest to a service provider tax-free, whereas receipt of an unrestricted stock interest in an S corporation by a service provider results in taxable income on its fair market value upon receipt.

LLCs also have a number of disadvantages compared to S corporations:

- Unlike the case with S or C corporations, if an LLC is purchased by another company, it is not possible to do a tax-free combination.

- Profits in an S corporation that are distributed to shareholder-employees may avoid some self-employment taxes (FICA and FUTA), whereas self-employment taxes on such profits in an LLC may be unavoidable for certain employees.

- LLCs are relatively recent creatures of state law, so the kind of developed, relatively uniform corporate law guidance that exists for S or C corporations is not available.

- Amounts attributable to inventory and accounts receivable in an LLC are taxed as ordinary income upon sale of the company; in an S corporation, they are taxed as capital gains.

- Most venture capital firms, because of restrictions imposed by their trust funds, cannot invest in LLCs. This is not the case with private equity firms, however, many of which are structured as LLCs.

Purchases or Gifts of Equity Interests in LLCs

The simplest approach is to have employees purchase an equity interest in the company. The question here is whether this really is an equity incentive rather than simply an employee investment. Some companies see the opportunity to buy ownership as an incentive, but many, if not most, employees will either not have the resources to make the investment, will decide other investments are more prudent (especially given the added taxes involved), or will have expectations resulting from the investment, such as a say in how the company is managed, that the other partners may not want to cede. Alternatively, employees can be granted an interest, but some owners think that unless employees have "skin in the game," they will not really act like owners (evidence in this is unclear).

Types of Equity Interests Available in LLCs

Where the company wants to award ownership interests to an employee, there are two primary types of equity interests available:

1. "Capital interests" give the owner a right to share in the value of LLC assets through the receipt of a share of the proceeds upon sale of the LLC assets.

2. "Profits interests" entitle the owner both to capital appreciation and profits of the business.

Either type of interest may be subject to restrictions, such as a vesting requirement that is satisfied by the employee's service for a specified period of time or by satisfaction of certain performance standards. Either type of interest may be forfeited if the employee engages in criminal activity that results in direct harm to the company, such as embezzlement. Many companies will also want employees to forfeit their interest if they go to work for competitors. While these anti-compete agreements can be written into grant agreements, they may be difficult to enforce.

The grant of either a capital or profits interest is a contractual matter. Companies need to have a written plan under which awards can be issued as well as individual agreements with employees detailing each party's rights and obligations (usually called an operating agreement). It is essential that these be developed by qualified counsel and that they define all terms and requirements unambiguously.

As noted in the previous chapter, another form of compensation that is common to many LLCs (particularly private equity and hedge funds) is the "carried interest," a perceived form of equity. Essentially, a carried interest is a profits interest. Although the carried interest is not actually equity in the LLC, it can be designed in a manner that provides the holder with an ongoing right to future income and that can be sold or otherwise transferred to others, depending on its terms and the operating agreement of the LLC.

Tax Consequences of Granting a Capital Interest in an LLC

An employee who receives a capital interest without a substantial risk of forfeiture (that is, a vested capital interest) in an LLC in exchange for services rendered recognizes compensation income in the year of the grant equal to the fair market value of the interest. The market value of this interest, for purposes of computing the employee's income and the LLC's deduction, may be determined in one of several ways: by reference to the value of the services rendered to the LLC's assets; by determining the value of the capital that was shifted from existing LLC members to the new grantee;[1] by determining the value according to what a willing buyer and willing seller would agree upon as a purchase price in an arm's-length sale (i.e., the willing buyer/willing seller test); or by determining the amount the employee would receive upon a liquidation of the LLC at the time the interest is issued (i.e., the liquidation value). Regardless of the method used to determine fair market value, income and employment tax withholding will be required.

If the interest is subject to a substantial risk of forfeiture and is nontransferable, then the taxable event can be delayed until the restriction lapses unless the employee makes a Section 83(b) election. A Section 83(b) election must be made by the employee within 30 days of the grant's award. The election states that the employee agrees to be taxed immediately upon receipt of the capital interest at ordinary income rates, with any subsequent appreciation in the interest taxed at capital gain rates upon disposition. An employee who receives a restricted capital interest will not be treated as a partner for tax purposes until the restriction lapses, unless the Section 83(b) election is made.

---

1.   An LLC will frequently "revalue" its assets immediately before the grant of a capital interest to a new member to prevent a "capital shift" of pre-grant appreciation of LLC assets in favor of the grantee. A shift in an LLC member's share of company liabilities would result in an increase in basis for the new owner's membership interest in the LLC.

If a Section 83(b) election is not made, then ordinary income tax is paid on the value of the award at the time it vests. Note that this is not the same as when the employee actually sells the capital interest, which may be later. Any difference between the price at vesting and the price at sale would be subject to long- or short-term capital gains taxes, depending on how long the capital interest is held.

The LLC is entitled to a deduction for the value of the capital interest that the employee reported as income at vesting or upon making the Section 83(b) election. Despite the fact that the capital interest is being exchanged for the employee's services, there is a risk that the LLC may still be required to recognize gain for a "deemed sale" consisting of the sale of an interest in its assets for cash, payment of the cash to the employee who rendered services to the LLC, and a subsequent contribution of the cash by the employee back to the LLC in exchange for the capital interest. Any gain resulting from the deemed sale would be taxable to the other LLC members but offset in part by a deduction for compensation paid to the employee.

Tax Consequences of Granting a Profits Interest in an LLC

Under an IRS-provided safe harbor, an employee's receipt of a profits interest in exchange for services is not taxable upon grant, even if the interest is fully vested, if each of the following three requirements are satisfied:[2]

1. The profits interest is received as a member or in anticipation of becoming a member;

2. The receipt of a profits interest is not related to a substantially certain and predictable stream of income; and

3. The interest is not sold within two years of receipt.

---

2. Revenue Procedure 93-27 and Revenue Procedure 2001-43. In May 2005, the IRS issued Notice 2005-43 and proposed Treasury regulations that would make Rev. Proc. 93-27 and Rev. Proc. 2001-43 obsolete. Until the new rules are finalized, Rev. Proc. 93-27 and Rev. Proc. 2001-43 will continue to apply.

There is no current deduction allowed to the other members of the LLC where the new member is not taxed on issuance of the profits interest.

If the safe harbor requirements are not satisfied, there is some uncertainty as to the employee's income tax consequences arising from the grant of a profits interest to an employee.

Where the profits interest is not vested at the time of grant, the employee will not be considered as the owner of the interest until it is fully vested unless a Section 83(b) election is made or the employee is treated as having made such an election (see below). If the employee cannot be treated as the owner of the interest, then the employee cannot be allocated profits or losses of the LLC until the interest vests. Once vested, however, the employee would be entitled to receive appreciation on the property for the period running between grant of the interest and its vesting unless there is an adjustment that allocates the built-in appreciation to existing members instead. It is worth noting that the receipt of an allocation of appreciation may convert the profits interest into a capital interest that is taxable at the time of vesting.

When the employee does redeem the profits interest, the gain is taxed as either short- or long-term capital gain.

How an employee should deal with making a Section 83(b) election is not entirely resolved, particularly in light of the IRS safe harbor, which allows for receipt of a vested profits interest to escape tax. IRS guidance has indicated that a restricted profits interest would be treated as received on the grant date rather than the vesting date if the recipient is treated as owner of the interest (receiving a distributive share of LLC items attributable to the interest) and the LLC does not claim a tax deduction for the value of the interest in the year it was granted or in the year it vests. In other words, the profits interest is treated as if a Section 83(b) election were made. As a result of this further guidance, there may no longer be a need to file a Section 83(b) election to include in the current year's income the value of a restricted profit interest, although many advisors would urge that an election be made anyway to protect against some unforeseen circumstance making this treatment inapplicable.

In addition, profits interest holders must receive a K-1 statement attributing their respective share of ownership to them. That means they will have a tax responsibility for the current income or gains of the LLC even though vesting rules for the award of LLC distribution policies do not entitle them to any distributions with which to pay these taxes. In an S corporation, distributions must be made pro-rata to owners, but, as noted above, this is not true in an LLC, so the LLC is not obligated to make sure the profits interest holder receives a distribution sufficient to pay taxes. Profits interest holders, of course, will want these "tax distributions." If they are paid, then they would be treated as advances against any future distributions to which the profits interest holder would be entitled.

Employees with profits interests are taxed as partners rather than employees, so their income is reported on a K-1 and is not subject to withholding. Holders must pay estimated income taxes on all their income from the LLC and self-employment taxes on salary.

Because a carried interest is the equivalent of a profits interest in the LLC, it has the same tax ramifications as the profits interest as discussed above. It should be noted that some LLCs use the term "carried interest," but in reality they are simply providing bonuses to employees. Each situation should be separately evaluated to determine whether the employee actually has a profits interest in the LLC.

Options to Acquire a Capital Interest or Profits Interest

As stated previously, there are two types of equity interests available in LLCs. However, as an alternative to the grant of an outright interest, LLCs can issue options to acquire either a capital interest or a profits interest. The advantage in doing so is that the grant of an option in such case is not taxable to the employee or to the LLC. An employee who exercises an option acquires an immediate interest in the underlying assets and future revenues of the LLC.

The exercise of an option on a capital interest will result in taxable income for the employee and a deduction for the LLC. The amount of taxable income equals the excess of the fair market value of the LLC interest received over the exercise price, if any. At exercise, the LLC would also need to address the "deemed sale" issue discussed previously.

The exercise of an option on a profits interest would not be taxable for the employee or LLC if the safe harbor rules are satisfied. At exercise, the appreciation in value issue discussed above would also need to be addressed.

Impact of Section 409A on Equity Interests in LLCs

Section 409A of the Internal Revenue Code requires deferred compensation plans with amounts deferred on or after January 1, 2005, to comply with various rules that are designed to place reasonable operational limits on the timing of an election to defer income as well as the events that entitle a participant to receive a plan distribution. This income tax provision was enacted in response to abuses perceived to have occurred in deferred compensation arrangements that had previously allowed many executives to determine the timing and form of payment from these plans. As a result of the enactment of Section 409A, virtually any plan, arrangement, or agreement that defers income tax on compensation is subject to its stringent requirements.

A failure to comply with either its documentation or operational requirements results in immediate income taxation on amounts previously deferred by plan participants as well as the assessment of 20% excise taxes and late payment interest. The IRS provides a procedure for correcting inadvertent operational errors, which generally involve either deferred amounts that should have been paid or amounts that should have been deferred.[3]

Although IRS Notice 2005-1[4] does not specifically mention LLCs, it states that Section 409A "is not limited to arrangements between an employer and employee" and "may apply to arrangements between a partner and a partnership which provides for the deferral of compensation under a nonqualified deferral compensation plan." The reference to partnerships should also apply to LLCs taxable as partnerships.

---

3.   The current version of this program appears in IRS Notice 2008-113.

4.   Section III.G of the preamble to the final regulations under Section 409A states that Notice 2005-1 continues to provide interim guidance regarding the application of Section 409A until further guidance is issued. There are many unresolved issues with respect to the application of Section 409A to transfers of compensatory interests in LLCs. Until such further needed guidance is issued, LLCs should strive to structure their equity arrangements to comply with Section 409A to the greatest extent possible.

As a result, Notice 2005-1 may be interpreted to permit taxpayers to treat the issuance of an equity interest (including a profits interest), or an option to purchase an equity interest, granted by an LLC in connection with the performance of services, under the same principles that govern the issuance of stock under Section 409A. A closer look at how such interests would be treated for 409A purposes follows.

Restricted and Unrestricted Capital Interests

In the context of LLC interests, Notice 2005-1 would permit the issuance of compensatory capital interest to be treated in the same manner as the issuance of stock, i.e., not resulting in the deferral of compensation because its value (and any subsequent income earned in respect of the capital interest) would be included in the recipient's income upon issuance. As such, the issuance and holding of a compensatory capital interest would be excluded from Section 409A's requirements. However, the receipt of a restricted capital interest (typically, one subject to a vesting schedule), is not a taxable event at the time of transfer (unless a Section 83(b) election has been made by the recipient).

It may be appropriate for Section 409A to apply to a transfer of a compensatory restricted capital interest, or a promise to deliver a capital interest in the future, where such interest or promise is not contingent on the performance of substantial future services, if the transfer or promise is considered to be a form of deferred compensation.

Profits Interests

Notice 2005-1 specifically exempts profits interests from Section 409A if the recipient of the profits interest is not required to include the value of the interest in income at the time of issuance under applicable guidance. Current tax guidance provides that neither the receipt nor vesting of a compensatory profits interest is a taxable event.[5] Since no income is recognized, none can be deferred under Section 409A.[6]

---

5. Once vested, the service provider recognizes income on his or her allocable share of the LLC's future income when earned.

6. Current rules do not address exemption of a profits interest from Section 409A where the profits interest has a readily ascertainable value at the time of grant.

LLC Options to Acquire Capital or Profits Interest and Equity Appreciation Rights

Notice 2005-1 provides that the treatment of compensatory issuances of LLC-based awards other than capital or profits interest may be governed, by analogy, under the Section 409A rules covering equity-based awards. Thus, the treatment of LLC options to acquire a capital or profits interest can be determined by reference to Section 409A's treatment of nonqualified stock options, and the treatment of LLC appreciation rights can be determined by reference to Section 409A's treatment of stock appreciation rights.

LLC Options to Acquire Capital or Profits Interest

Notice 2005-1 states that the grant of a nonqualified stock option with respect to stock of a service recipient does not result in a deferral of compensation, and therefore avoids Section 409A, only if (1) the option exercise price is never less than the fair market value of the underlying stock on the grant date; (2) the receipt, transfer, or exercise of the option is subject to taxation under Section 83; and (3) the option does not include any additional deferral features. It may be impractical in certain circumstances to value LLC assets in connection with each option grant, due to the intangible or illiquid nature of the assets involved. For this reason, an LLC interested in issuing option grants may wish to do so when other valuation events occur.

If the Section 409A requirements applicable to nonqualified stock options are not satisfied with respect to an option to acquire an LLC capital or profits interest, the option holder would likely recognize income upon option vesting equal to the excess of the fair market value of the LLC interest underlying the option over the amount of the exercise price, plus the additional 20% tax with interest under Section 409A.

LLC Equity Appreciation Rights

Notice 2005-1 provides that stock appreciation rights are treated as deferral compensation subject to Section 409A unless (1) the rights relate to the stock of a service recipient, (2) the exercise price of the right is equal to fair market value of the stock on the date of grant, (3) the right settles only in stock, (4) the stock is traded on an established securities exchange, and (5) the right does not contain any additional deferral features. Using the foregoing criteria, LLC appreciation rights granted by most privately held LLCs would be subject to Section 409A because such LLC appreciation rights could not satisfy the "publicly traded" requirement.

It is possible for an LLC appreciation right to comply with Section 409A's requirements if the exercise date of such an appreciation right is fixed as of the grant date. In such a case, the appreciation right may provide that exercise will occur on the earlier of a date certain or termination of employment.

Earned Income and Availability of Tax-Favored Fringe Benefits

Not all LLC members may be treated for income tax purposes as common law employees. As such, only LLC members who are providing a service to the company, and thus receive earned income, may—but not always will—be considered for tax-favored treatment with respect to the company's benefit programs.

One example involves the income tax rules governing supplemental unemployment benefit (SUB) trusts, which provide that a service member of an LLC may not receive benefits from a SUB plan unless such individual is classified as an "employee" under the state or federal unemployment compensation laws covering employment.[7] Members who are compensated for services through guaranteed payments, considered to be earned income, will qualify to deduct 100% of their health insurance premiums to the extent of their pro-rata share of net profits.[8] The members' share of net profits is not considered earned income, and therefore inactive members who receive solely a distribution of profits will not qualify for the health insurance premium deduction.

---

7.   Treas. Reg. §1.501(c)(17)-1(b)(2).

8.   Guaranteed payments are defined in Treas. Reg. §1.707-1(c) and understood as "payments made by a partnership to a partner for services." As such, these payments are treated as self-employment income and therefore render the recipient eligible for deduction of his or her self-employed health insurance expenses.

Expert Advice Required

Due to their relative flexibility, LLCs may develop equity plans that fit their business objectives and align the interests of employees with the company to promote further growth of the enterprise. Taxed at capital gain rates, the capital interest or profits interest may provide the incentive needed for employees while minimizing dilution of ownership in the company. However, the limited guidance issued in this area poses unique challenges that must be handled with skill by an experienced advisor.

While it is always important to have expert advice on any equity plan, the complexity of the tax treatment that equity incentives in LLCs involve, as well as the more difficult planning issues, makes it even more important to engage people who know the field very well.

CHAPTER 4

ACCOUNTING FOR EQUITY COMPENSATION IN AN LLC

Alan Nadel

The limited liability company (LLC) has become a common form of business organization in the U.S. only within the past 20 years. While those who establish accounting standards have paid much attention to equity compensation, their focus has been primarily on corporations rather than other forms of legal entities, such as LLCs. It has been quite common for decades to provide equity interests to employees, particularly executives, as a means of providing incentive and long-term compensation. Because LLCs have been introduced only recently, the accounting literature applicable to equity compensation does not specifically address these types of entities. Nevertheless, the general language of the relevant accounting literature makes clear that it is appropriate to apply the same equity compensation accounting rules to other entities as are applicable to corporations.

Before getting into the specific rules applicable to equity compensation, it is first important to identify which set of rules we should be looking to. In the United States, accounting for business transactions is covered under generally accepted accounting principles (GAAP). Virtually any transaction in American business is specifically addressed by one (and sometimes more than one) GAAP rule, including those for executive and employee pay programs. GAAP guidelines are developed primarily by the Financial Accounting Standards Board (FASB). All companies in the United States must follow GAAP regardless of whether they are publicly traded.

The FASB derives its authority from the Sarbanes-Oxley Act and the Securities and Exchange Commission (SEC). It is an independent board but receives significant input from the SEC. Outside the United States, accounting rules generally are established by the International Accounting Standards Board (IASB). The IASB establishes international financial reporting standards (IFRS) that have been adopted in almost 110 countries around the world. There has been considerable discussion in the United States about possibly transitioning U.S. accounting standards from GAAP to IFRS sometime within the next few years. Whether this is conjecture or will eventually come to be, U.S. companies continue to be subject to the rules of GAAP; therefore, this discussion of relevant accounting principles will fall under the rules of GAAP. It should be noted, however, that while the rules of IFRS are similar to those of GAAP, notable differences exist between the two and may affect company stock-based programs if the U.S. eventually moves to IFRS.

Before 1995, the applicable accounting rules for equity compensation in the United States were dictated by Accounting Principles Board Opinion No. 25, *Accounting for Stock Issued to Employees* ("APB 25"). Recognizing that those accounting rules were developed for the simpler equity compensation programs of the early 1970s, the FASB decided to develop more comprehensive rules for equity compensation programs. It issued Statement of Financial Accounting Standards No. 123, *Accounting for Stock-Based Compensation* ("FAS 123"), in 1995. However, under pressure from the business community, the FASB drafted FAS 123 to allow employers to choose whether they used the accounting of APB 25 or FAS 123. Most companies chose to continue using the older accounting rules under APB 25, whereby no expense was recognized for most stock options, and simply disclose the effect of FAS 123 in the financial statement footnotes. When the economic environment changed significantly, the FASB revised the 1995 rules and made them mandatory for all companies under rules issued in late 2004, Statement of Financial Accounting Standards No. 123 (revised 2004), *Share-Based Payment* ("FAS 123R").[1]

Applicable Accounting

The rules of FAS 123R make significant changes to the accounting practices that almost all companies were following until 2005. Unlike the intrinsic value rules of APB 25, FAS 123R requires that the "fair value" of all equity compensation awards be recognized as an expense. The rules of FAS 123R

1. As this book went to press, FASB was introducing a codification of all U.S. accounting standards. Although the new numbering system may change the references to FAS 123R, the rules discussed in this chapter will remain the same.

are different from those under current GAAP for recognizing the cost of other assets and liabilities. Some of these changes are:

- Use of special valuation models for determining the cost of employee options to purchase employer equity
- Accrual patterns for recognizing the expense associated with vested awards
- Accounting treatment for recognizing the income tax effects of equity awards
- Impact of performance-vested awards
- Modifications and other changes to outstanding equity awards

Although the rules of FAS 123R are geared toward corporate stock programs, they are just as relevant for equity interests that are granted to LLC employees. Not surprisingly, certain adjustments must be made. In some LLC companies, employees are allowed to purchase an equity interest in the LLC. If the cost of that capital interest in the LLC is on similar terms (e.g., price) as for other investors in the LLC, then the employee's capital interest would most likely not be treated as a compensatory one. FAS 123R would not be applicable, and the LLC would recognize no compensation expense. On the other hand, the grant (at little or no cost) of a capital interest in the LLC would be subject to the expense recognition rules of FAS 123R.

As discussed in previous sections, employees in an LLC frequently receive a profits interest in the company rather than a capital interest. This allows the employees to share in the profits of the business and receive an annual cash payment rather than gain an ownership interest in the company that may increase in value over time. As discussed further below, the accounting for a profits interest generally is different from that for a capital interest.

Measurement

The first step in determining the accounting for an LLC interest is to measure the total amount of that expense. This may differ among the various types of LLC ownership interests, which are discussed in chapters 2 and 3 of this book.

Capital Interest

A capital interest in an LLC is similar to restricted stock in a corporation. In both cases the employee has an ownership interest in the capital or equity of the organization. Consequently, the accounting for both is similar. The employer must recognize an expense for the fair value of the capital interest that the employee is receiving for services rendered. In the case of a publicly traded corporation or LLC, this is the traded value of the stock or unit as determined by the public markets. Because most LLCs are privately held, however, determining fair value is more difficult. One indicator of fair value would be a reference to a recent similar transaction for a capital interest that was purchased by an unrelated third party. In the absence of such a purchase, it may be necessary to obtain an appraisal or other determination of value from an independent professional. In some cases, it may be helpful to establish a formula value that would be used for purposes of buying and selling capital interests in the LLC.

In 2004 the American Institute of Certified Public Accountants (AICPA) issued a Practice Aid to guide privately held companies with the valuation of their equity securities issued for purposes of employee compensation. The AICPA Practice Aid indicates that the valuation of these equity securities should be conducted using any of three acceptable valuation methods:

- Market-based
- Income-based (e.g., discounted cash flows)
- Asset-based

Although independent appraisers have used other commonly accepted valuation methods, only these three meet the guidelines established in the Practice Aid. Also, although all of the methodologies detailed in the Practice Aid are used by valuation specialists, the Practice Aid indicates a preference for different methods based on various characteristics or other criteria specific to each company's circumstances.

Furthermore, the Practice Aid provides a hierarchy of valuation methodologies to indicate a preference for the type of valuation private companies should use. Preferably, the valuation should be conducted contemporaneously with the issuance of the compensatory equity by an unrelated valuation specialist. If that is not possible, the next preferred approach is a retrospective valuation by an unrelated valuation specialist. The least preferred method for valuing the securities is a valuation established by a "related party valuation specialist."

Valuations that are performed along the guidelines detailed in the AICPA Practice Aid will be more likely to meet the approval of the company's auditors. With respect to private companies that undergo an initial public offering (IPO), the SEC has accepted valuations of employee equity using the AICPA Practice Aid and has not challenged these valuations. This is a significant departure from the SEC's previous practice of challenging the valuation of employee equity issued in the year prior to an IPO under its "cheap stock" theory. This often resulted in companies recognizing an additional compensation expense at the time of the IPO in order to gain SEC approval. Instead, companies following the guidelines of the AICPA Practice Aid for the valuation of employee equity will not be challenged by the SEC in this regard.

Option to Purchase Capital Interest

The grant of an option to purchase a capital interest in the LLC will be treated similarly to a stock option, which allows an employee to buy corporate stock at a time of his or her choosing and at agreed-upon terms. Unlike the previous rules of APB 25, FAS 123R requires the use of special valuation models for determining the value of the option. The LLC may choose to use a closed-form valuation model (e.g., Black-Scholes) or an open-form approach such as the binomial model. The FASB has no preference which formula the employer chooses, provided that it is applied consistently. Most companies use the Black-Scholes formulation because of its simplicity. Both approaches require the use of six valuation assumptions:

- Fair value of the underlying equity (e.g., capital interest)
- Exercise price of the option
- Life or term of the option
- Prevailing risk-free interest rate

- Volatility of the price of the underlying capital interest
- Dividend yields of the capital interest, if any

Each of these assumptions must be calculated or estimated by the company. Under the Black-Scholes approach, each of the valuation factors is assumed to remain constant throughout the life of the option. In contrast, the open-form model allows the employer to assume that the valuation assumptions will change over the life of the option as well as to consider other factors (e.g., employee turnover) that may affect the value of the option.

Each of the valuation assumptions is determined for an LLC similarly to the way it would be for a corporation. The most difficult one, however, is the determination of volatility. Assuming the LLC is a privately held company, it is difficult or impractical to measure the expected volatility of an LLC unit. Instead, the LLC is required to measure its options to purchase a capital interest based on a value determined by using the historical volatility of an appropriate industry sector index instead of the expected volatility of an LLC unit price.

Profits Interest

Unlike the capital interest in an LLC, a profits interest provides only for a share of future net income of the LLC. Although the terms of the profits interest may allow the employee to sell his or her interest in the LLC, it does not represent any ownership of the underlying capital or equity of the company. It is merely a right to a future cash payment based on company profits. FAS 123R addresses situations in which employee awards are settled in cash rather than an ownership interest in the business. It specifically provides for liability accounting in such cases.

The accounting rules allow the private company to make a "policy decision" about how to account for liability awards. The company may use either fair value or intrinsic value for award valuation purposes. Regardless of which approach is used, the profits interest is valued at the grant date (similar to the treatment of capital interests). Furthermore, in each subsequent accounting period the profits interest is subject to mark-to-market treatment until the award is settled. The result is that the company recognizes an expense for all cash payments made to the employee while he or she holds the profits interest rather than fixing the expense at the initial date of grant.

Carried Interest

As noted in Chapter 2, another form of compensation that is common to many LLCs (particularly private equity and hedge funds) is the "carried interest," a perceived form of equity. A carried interest provides the employee with the right to share in the profits of the LLC, similar to a profits interest. In some cases a carried interest is nothing more than a bonus arrangement, whereas in others it may entitle the employee to a predetermined portion of the LLC profits, calculated after all expenses have been paid. Although the carried interest is not actually equity in the LLC, it can be designed in a manner that provides the holder with an ongoing right to future income and that can be sold or otherwise transferred to others, depending on its terms and the LLC's operating agreement.

LLC Equity Appreciation Rights

As discussed above, phantom LLC units track periodic profits distributed by the LLC, similar to stock appreciation rights in a corporation. The employee receives no LLC ownership interest other than the right to receive periodic cash payments. Consequently, LLC equity appreciation rights will be accounted for in the same manner as profits interests using liability accounting.

Compensation Expense Accruals

Once the amount of compensation expense has been determined under equity accounting, the aggregate expense must be amortized over the employee's service period. This is usually the same as the vesting period. If the vesting occurs all at the end of the service period, the total expense is amortized on a level (straight-line) basis so that the same amount of expense is recognized each year during the service period.

If the employee partially vests each year during the service period, the employer may choose either straight-line or multiple-option amortization. By using the multiple-option approach, the amount of the expense to be recognized each year is treated as a separate award and amortized accordingly. For example an award that vests ratably over three years is treated as a grant of three separate awards: an award vesting in one year, an award vesting in two years, and an award vesting in three years. Each year's award is expensed over its appropriate vesting period. The net result is an expense in the first year consisting of 100% of the first year's award, plus 50% of the second year's award, plus 33% of the third year's award.

Vesting Conditions

The basis for determining an employee's vesting in the award may affect the amount of expense recognized for that award. If the vesting is based on service or performance conditions, no compensation expense is recognized for awards that are forfeited as a result of termination of employment or performance conditions not achieved. Forfeitures are estimated at the time of grant, and the estimate is eventually trued up based on actual experience during the vesting period. Additionally, compensation expense attributable to forfeited awards is reversed in the period of forfeiture.

If the vesting is based on the value of the LLC, no adjustments are made for forfeitures. Because the typical LLC is not publicly traded, this provision is seldom seen in LLC awards.

Income Tax Benefit

If the nature of an award is expected to produce a tax deduction for the LLC, the benefit of that tax deduction must be taken into account in determining the net cost of the equity award. Because of the differences in the timing of an expense of an award (at grant) and the tax deduction for that award (vesting, exercise, or payout), determining the relevant amounts of the future tax deductions is more complicated. The tax benefit is calculated based on the grant date value of the equity award and the company's effective tax rate.

The LLC must establish a pool of unused tax benefits that would have been recognized under FAS 123 between 1995 and 2005. Furthermore, any additional tax benefits that arise after 2005 and are not included in income (see next paragraph) are added to the pool.

If the ultimate tax benefit is greater than the expected tax benefit, the surplus is credited to capital in the balance sheet. Also, it is included in the pool of unused tax benefits (see previous paragraph). It does not flow through the income statement and thus is not included in net income or earnings per share. If the actual tax benefit is less than the expected tax benefit, the shortfall reduces the pool of unused tax benefits and need not be taken into account as an expense. If things reach a point where no surplus tax benefits remain in the pool, the remaining shortfall is charged to earnings as additional income tax expense.

Modifications

In the event that an award is subsequently modified, it is treated as the exchange of the original award for a new equity award. A modification is deemed to occur when there is a change in any of the award's terms or conditions. An additional compensation expense must be recognized for any incremental fair value of the new award over the fair value of the canceled award. Additionally, any remaining unrecognized compensation cost from the date of grant must also be recognized. Unlike the case with previous accounting rules, determinations of change in value must be measured in terms of fair value rather than intrinsic value. The measurement of additional compensation expense is based on the fair value of the equity award immediately before the modification and immediately after the modification. In no event will the total compensation cost be less than the fair value at the date of grant. Some examples of modifications are:

- Exchanges of equity awards relating to a business combination or in equity restructuring
- Inducements to terminate employment or retire early
- Cash-out of all award values, to the extent payment exceeds the fair value of the award immediately before the cash-out
- Repricing of an equity instrument

CHAPTER 5

A Primer on Sharing Equity with Employees in Non-LLC Companies

Corey Rosen

This book focuses on equity compensation plans for limited liability companies, but it is important to understand equity compensation in the context of C or S corporations as well for two reasons. First, if you do a Web search for equity compensation plans in LLCs, most of the articles will say that it is a lot easier and often recommended to switch to S or C status instead because the rules and alternative approaches are simpler and more certain. Second, the concepts of sharing equity in an LLC generally parallel concepts in an S or C corporation. By understanding these more familiar concepts, it may be easier to see how their equivalents in LLCs work.

For most LLCs that decide to convert, an S corporation is the logical choice. The tax treatment of S corporations and LLCs is similar in many ways. Both are pass-through entities, meaning there is no corporate level tax. Instead, individual owners pay taxes on any profits and gains. While there are a number of differences, the key difference is that in an S corporation, distributions must be proportional to ownership, whereas an LLC can make distributions in other ways if it so chooses.

The first part of this chapter looks at individual equity plans; these plans can be used for selective or broad-based plans. The second part looks at plans that are designed to benefit most or all employees. This chapter focuses on plan design and tax issues. Securities law considerations are briefly discussed in a separate section, but because this is such a complex subject, they are not reviewed in any detail. Accounting issues are extremely complex and varied for different plans and are discussed only briefly here. For more information on accounting concerns, see the NCEO's books *Accounting for Equity-Based Compensation* (for individual equity plans and employee stock purchase plans) or *Leveraged ESOPs and Employee Buyouts* (for ESOPs).

Basic Forms of Individual Equity Plans

There are four basic kinds of individual equity compensation plans: stock options, restricted stock and restricted stock units, stock appreciation rights, and phantom stock. Many of these plans have variations as well. Each plan provides employees with some special consideration in price or terms. (This chapter does not cover simply offering employees the right to buy stock on the same terms any other investor would receive, or making unrestricted grants of shares.)

Stock options give employees the right to buy a number of shares at a price fixed at grant for a defined number of years into the future. *Restricted stock* (and its close relative *restricted stock units*) give employees the right to acquire or receive shares, by gift or purchase, once certain restrictions, such as working a certain number of years or meeting a performance target, are met. *Phantom stock* pays a future cash bonus equal to the value of a certain number of shares. *Stock appreciation rights* provide the right to the increase in the value of a designated number of shares, usually paid in cash, but occasionally settled in shares (this is called a "stock-settled SAR").

Stock Options

A few key concepts help define how stock options work:

- *Exercise:* The purchase of stock with an option.
- *Exercise price:* The price at which the stock can be purchased. This is also called the *strike price*. In most plans, the exercise price is the current fair market value of the stock at the time the exercise is made.
- *Grant price:* How much the option holder must pay to exercise the option.
- *Spread:* The difference between the grant price and exercise price at the time of exercise.
- *Option term:* The amount of time the employee can hold the option before it expires.

- *Vesting*: The requirement, usually in years of service, that must be met for an option holder to be able to exercise an option.

A company grants an employee options to buy a stated number of shares at a defined grant price. The options vest over a period of time or once certain individual, group, or corporate goals are met. Once vested, the employee can exercise the option at the grant price at any time over the option term up to the expiration date. For instance, an employee might be granted the right to buy 1,000 shares at $10 per share. The options vest 25% per year over four years and have a term of 10 years. If the stock goes up, the employee will pay $10 per share to buy the stock. The difference between the $10 grant price and the exercise price is the spread. If the stock goes to $25 after seven years, and the employee exercises all options, the spread would be $15 per share.

Kinds of Options

Employee stock options are either incentive stock options (ISOs) or nonqualified options (NSOs). When an employee exercises a nonqualified stock option, the spread on exercise is taxable to the employee as ordinary income, even if the shares are not yet sold. A corresponding amount is deductible by the company. There is no legally required holding period for the shares after exercise, although the company may impose one. Any subsequent gain or loss on the shares after exercise is taxed as capital gains or losses.

An incentive stock option (ISO) enables an employee to (1) defer taxation on the option from the date of exercise until the date of sale of the underlying shares and (2) to pay tax at capital gains rates, rather than ordinary income tax rates, on the spread at exercise. Certain conditions must be met to qualify for ISO treatment:

1. The employee must hold the stock for at least one year after the exercise date or two years after the grant date, whichever is later.

2. Only $100,000 of stock options can become exercisable in any year. This is measured by the grant price of the options, not the exercise price. It means that only $100,000 in grant price value can vest (first become exercisable) in any one year. If there is overlapping vesting,

such as would occur if options are granted annually and vest gradually, companies must track outstanding options to see if the amount
that becomes vested under different grants would exceed $100,000
in grant value in any one year. Any amount exceeding $100,000 is
treated as coming from an NSO.

3. The exercise price must be equal to at least 100% of the market price
of the company's stock on the date of the grant.

4. Only employees can qualify for an ISO.

5. The option must be granted pursuant to a written plan that has
been approved by shareholders, that specifies how many shares can
be issued under the plan, and that identifies the class of employees
eligible to receive the options. Options must be granted within 10
years of the date of the adoption of the plan.

6. The option cannot by its terms be exercisable more than 10 years
after the date of the grant.

7. The employee cannot own, at the time of the grant, more than 10%
of the voting power of all outstanding stock of the company, unless
the exercise price is at least 110% of the market value of the stock
on the date of the grant, and the option is not exercisable more than
five years from the date of the grant.

If all the rules for incentive options are met at the time of exercise,
then the transaction is called a "qualifying disposition," and the employee
pays capital gains tax on the total increase in value at sale over the grant
price. However, the spread on the option at exercise is a "preference item"
for purposes of the alternative minimum tax (AMT). So even though
the shares may not have been sold, the exercise requires the employee to
add back the gain on exercise, along with other AMT preference items,
to see if an alternative minimum tax payment is due.

The company does not take a tax deduction when there is a qualifying
disposition. If, however, there is a disqualifying disposition, most often
because the employee exercises and sells before meeting the required
holding periods, the spread on exercise is taxable to the employee at ordinary income tax rates, and any capital appreciation on the ISO shares
in excess of the market price on exercise of an ISO is taxed at capital

gains rates. In this instance, the company may then deduct the spread on exercise.

Exercising an Option

There are four ways to exercise a stock option: cash, the exchange of existing shares (often called a stock swap), same-day sales, and their close relative, sell-to-cover sales (these latter two are often called cashless exercises, although that term actually includes other kinds of exercise methods described here as well). Any one company, however, may provide for just one or two of these alternatives. Private companies do not offer same-day or sell-to-cover sales, and they often restrict the exercise or sale of the shares acquired through exercise until the company is sold or goes public.

The most common form of exercise for an option in a closely held company is simply for the employee to pay cash for the shares. The employee might then have additional taxes due, depending on the kind of option. If the options are nonqualified, the employer might then have to withhold taxes on the spread from the employee's future paychecks, unless the employer can arrange to use some of the option shares to pay for this obligation, as would normally be the case in the kind of cashless transactions described below.

In a same-day sale, the employee works with a broker, usually one provided by the company. The company provides the broker with enough shares to cover the option exercise, the broker turns around and sells them, and the proceeds, minus the exercise price and any taxes due, go to the employee. Although called a "same-day" sale, the process can take up to three days. In a sell-to-cover exercise, the same approach is used, but the broker sells only enough shares to cover the exercise price and any taxes due, giving the employee the remaining value in shares.

In a stock swap, the employee simply exchanges existing shares for the option shares. For instance, if the employee has the right to buy 1,000 shares at $10 per share and the shares are now worth $25, the employee would exchange 400 shares the employee currently owns for the 1,000 shares. That's because the 400 shares the employee owns are worth $10,000. The employee would then get 600 shares from the option. If there are taxes due as well, then the employee might choose to turn in enough shares to cover the taxes as well, although this is not a common strategy. Stock swaps are more commonly used with incentive stock options where taxes do not have to be paid until the newly acquired shares are sold.

Accounting

Under rules for equity compensation plans that became effective in 2006, companies must calculate the present value of all option awards as of the date of grant and show this as a charge to compensation. The value should be adjusted based on vesting experience (so unvested shares do not count as a charge to compensation).

Restricted Stock

Restricted stock provides the employee with the right to purchase shares at fair market value or a discount, or simply grants shares to employees outright. However, the shares employees acquire are not really theirs yet—they cannot take possession of the shares until specified restrictions lapse. Most commonly, the restriction is that the employee work for the company for a certain number of years, often three to five. The time-based restrictions may pass all at once or gradually. Any restrictions could be imposed, however. The company could, for instance, restrict the shares until certain corporate, departmental, or individual performance goals are achieved. With restricted stock units (RSUs), employees do not actually buy or receive shares *until* the restrictions lapse. In effect, RSUs are like phantom stock settled in shares instead of cash.

While the shares are subject to restrictions, companies can choose whether to pay dividends, provide voting rights, or give the employee other benefits of being a shareholder. When employees are awarded the restricted stock, they have the right to make what is called an "Section 83(b)" election. If they make the election, they are taxed at ordinary income tax rates on the "bargain element" of the award at the time of grant. If the shares are simply granted to the employee, then the bargain element is their full value. If some consideration is paid, then the tax is based on the difference between what is paid and the fair market value at the time of the grant. If full price is paid, there is no tax. Any future increase in the value of the shares until they are sold is then taxed as capital gains, not ordinary income. If employees do not make the election, then there is no tax until the restrictions lapse, at which time ordinary income tax is due on the difference between the grant and exercise price. Subsequent changes in value are capital gains (or losses). Employees cannot make the Section 83(b) election for RSUs.

The employer gets a tax deduction only for amounts employees pay income tax on, regardless of whether a Section 83(b) election is made or not. A Section 83(b) election carries some risk. If the employee makes the election and pays tax, but the restrictions never lapse, the employee does not get the taxes paid refunded, nor does the employee get the shares.

Restricted stock accounting parallels option accounting in most respects. If the only restriction is vesting, companies account for restricted stock by first determining the total compensation cost at the time the award is made. So if the employee is simply given 1,000 restricted shares worth $10 per share, then a $10,000 cost is incurred. If the employee buys the shares at fair value, no charge is recorded; if there is a discount, that counts as a cost. The cost is then amortized over the period of vesting until the restrictions lapse. Because the accounting is based on the initial cost, companies with a low share price will find that a vesting requirement for the award means their accounting charge will be very low even if the stock price goes up.

If the award is more contingent, such as performance vesting, the value must be adjusted each year for the current stock price, then amortized over the estimated life of the award (the time estimated to meet the performance goal). Each year, the expected cost is amortized over the estimated remaining expected life. So if the stock is awarded at $10 and goes to $15 in the first year of an expected five-year term, then $15 x 1,000 x .20 is recorded ($3,000). If the price goes to $18 the next year, the calculation is $18 x 1,000 x .40 ($3,600). The prior $2,000 is subtracted from this amount, yielding a charge of $1,800 for that year.

Phantom Stock and Stock Appreciation Rights

Stock appreciation rights (SARs) and phantom stock are very similar plans. Both essentially are cash bonus plans, although some plans pay out the benefits in the form of shares. SARs typically provide the employee with a cash payment based on the increase in the value of a stated number of shares over a specific period of time. Phantom stock provides a cash or stock bonus based on the value of a stated number of shares, to be paid out at the end of a specified period of time. SARs may not have a specific settlement date; like options, the employees may have flexibility in when to choose to exercise the SAR. Phantom stock may pay dividends; SARs generally do not. When the payout is made, it is taxed as ordinary income to the employee and is deductible to the employer. Some phantom plans condition the receipt of the award on meeting certain objectives, such as sales, profits, or other targets. These plans often call their phantom stock "performance units."

Because SARs and phantom plans are essentially cash bonuses or are delivered in the form of stock that holders will want to cash in, companies need to figure out how to pay for them. Does the company just make a promise to pay or does it really put aside the funds? If the award is paid in stock, is there a market for the stock? If it is only a promise, will employees believe the benefit is as phantom as the stock? If it is in real funds set aside for this purpose, the company will be putting after-tax dollars aside instead of using them in the business. Many small, growth-oriented companies cannot afford to do this. The fund can also be subject to excess accumulated earnings tax. On the other hand, if employees are given shares, the shares can be paid for by capital markets if the company goes public or by acquirers if the company is sold.

If phantom stock or SARs are irrevocably promised to employees, it is possible the benefit will become taxable before employees actually receive the funds. A "rabbi trust," a segregated account to fund deferred payments to employees, may help solve the accumulated earnings problem, but if the company is unable to pay creditors with existing funds, the money in these trusts goes to them. Telling employees their right to the benefit is not irrevocable, or is dependent on some condition (working another five years, for instance), may prevent the money from being currently taxable, but it may also weaken employee belief that the benefit is real.

Finally, if phantom stock or SARs are intended to benefit most or all employees and defer some or all payment until termination or later, they may be considered a de facto "ERISA plan." ERISA (the Employee Retirement Income and Security Act of 1974) is the federal law that governs retirement plans. It does not allow non-ERISA plans to operate like ERISA plans, so the plan could be ruled subject to all the constraints of ERISA. Similarly, if there is an explicit or implied reduction in compensation to get the phantom stock, there could be securities issues involved, most likely anti-fraud disclosure requirements. Plans designed just for a limited number of employees, or as a bonus for a broader group of employees that pays out annually based on a measure of equity, would most likely avoid these problems. Moreover, the regulatory issues are "gray areas"; it could be that a company could use a broad-based plan that pays over longer periods or at departure and not ever be challenged.

Phantom stock and SAR accounting is straightforward. These plans are treated in the same way as deferred cash compensation. As the amount of the liability changes each year, an entry is made for the amount accrued. A decline in value would create a negative entry. These entries are not contingent on vesting. In closely held companies, share value is often stated as book value. However, this can dramatically underrate the true value of a company, especially one based primarily on intellectual capital. Having an outside appraisal performed, therefore, can make the plans much more accurate rewards for employee contributions.

Employee Stock Purchase Plans

Millions of employees become owners in their companies through employee stock purchase plans (ESPPs). Many of these plans are organized under Section 423 of the tax code and thus are often called "Section 423" plans. Other ESPPs are "nonqualified" plans, meaning they do not have to meet the special rules of Section 423 and do not get any of the special tax treatment.

Under Section 423, companies must allow all employees to participate but can exclude those with less than two years' tenure, part-time employees, and highly compensated employees. All employees must have the same rights and privileges under the plan, although companies can allow purchase limits to vary with relative compensation (most do not do this, however). Plans can limit how much employees can buy, and the law limits it to $25,000 per year.

Section 423 plans operate by allowing employees to have deductions taken out of their pay on an after-tax basis. These deductions accumulate over an "offering period." At a specified time or times employees can choose to use these accumulated deductions to purchase shares, or they can get the money back. Plans can offer discounts of up to 15% on the price of the stock. Most plans allow this discount to be taken based on *either* the price at the beginning or end of the offering period (the so-called "look-back feature"). The offering period can last up to five years if the price employees pay for their stock is based on the share price at the end of the period or 27 months if it can be determined at an earlier point.

Plan design can vary in a number of ways. For instance, a company might allow employees a 15% discount on the price at the end of the offering period, but no discount if they buy shares based on the price at the beginning of the period. Some companies offer employees interim opportunities to buy shares during the offering period. Others provide smaller discounts. Offering periods also vary in length. NCEO studies, however, show that the large majority of plans have a look-back feature and provide 15% discounts off the share price at the beginning or end of the offering period. Most of the plans have a 12-month offering period, with six months the next most common.

The tax treatment of a Section 423 plan is similar to that of an incentive stock option plan. If employees hold the shares for two years after grant and one year after exercise, they pay ordinary income tax on the lesser of (1) the discount element as of the beginning of the offering period and (2) the amount by which the sale price exceeds the purchase price. Any additional gain is taxed as a long-term capital gain. The company gets no tax deduction, even on the discount. There is no withholding requirement on the gain on the employee purchase of shares.

If these rules are not met, employees pay ordinary income tax on the difference between the exercise price and the fair market value of the stock on the purchase date, plus long-term or short-term capital gains taxes on any increase in value over the purchase price. The company gets a tax deduction for the spread between the purchase price and the exercise price.

Nonqualified ESPPs usually work much the same way, but there are no rules for how they must be structured and no special tax benefits. The employee would pay tax on the discount as ordinary income *at the time the stock is purchased* and would pay capital gains on any subsequent gain.

ESPPs are found almost exclusively in public companies because the offering of stock to employees requires compliance with costly and complex securities laws. Closely held companies can, and sometimes do, have these plans, however. Offerings of stock only to employees can qualify for an exemption from securities registration requirements at the federal level, although they will have to comply with anti-fraud disclosure rules and, possibly, state securities laws as well. If they do offer stock in a stock purchase plan, it is highly advisable to obtain at least an annual appraisal.

ESPPs are very popular in public companies and some pre-IPO companies (where the plan starts before the IPO, and purchases are not made until after it) as they offer a benefit to employees and additional capital to companies. Any dilution resulting from the issuance of new shares to satisfy the purchase requests, or from the company repurchasing outstanding shares and reselling them at a discount, is usually so small that shareholders do not object. Rates of participation vary widely, with the median levels around 30% to 40% of eligible employees. Because most employees do not commit large amounts to these plans, and many do not participate at all, ESPPs should generally be seen as an adjunct to other employee ownership plans, not a means in themselves to create an ownership culture.

ESPPs are accounted for in the same way as options. Any discount offered counts as a compensation charge, and the present value of the option element must be calculated as an additional charge to income.

Securities Law Issues

If employees are given a right to purchase shares, the offer is subject to securities laws. The two key elements of securities laws are registration and disclosure. Registration means the filing of documents with the state and/or federal securities agencies concerning the employer whose stock is being sold. There are registration procedures for small offerings of stock (under $1 million or $5 million, depending on the procedure) that can be done for relatively small legal fees (as little as $10,000 in some cases), but larger offerings require a lot of complex paperwork, and fees often exceed $100,000. Registration requires the filing of audited financial statements and continuing reporting obligations to the federal Securities and Exchange Commission (SEC) and appropriate state agencies.

Disclosure refers to providing information to buyers about what they are getting, similar to, but frequently less detailed than, what would be in a prospectus. At times, there are specific state and federal rules about what needs to go in these documents, including objective discussions of risks, the financial condition of the firm, officers' and directors' salaries, and other information. In the absence of requirements for the registration of the securities, disclosure is intended to satisfy the anti-fraud requirements of federal and state laws.

Generally, offers to sell securities (stocks, bonds, etc.) require registration of those securities unless there is a specific exemption. In addition, companies with 500 or more shareholders and more than $10 million in assets are considered public firms under federal law and must comply with the reporting requirements of the Exchange Act of 1934 even if they do not have to register under the Securities Act of 1933. (An exemption added by the SEC in 2007 allows companies to exclude holders of unexercised compensatory employee stock options from the 500-shareholder calculation if the company otherwise does not have to report under the Exchange Act.)

There are a number of exemptions from these rules listed below. These are exemptions from registration; any time stock is offered, it should include appropriate financial disclosure to satisfy anti-fraud rules.

The most important of these exemptions is Rule 701. Under federal law, offers to a company's employees, directors, general partners, trustees, officers, or certain consultants (those providing services to a company similar to what an employer might hire someone to do, but not consultants who help raise capital) can be made under a written compensation agreement. If total sales during a 12-month period do not exceed the greater of: $1 million, 15% of the issuer's total assets, or 15% of all the outstanding securities of that class, then the offerings are exempt from registration requirements. The offerings must be discrete (not included in any other offer) and are still subject to disclosure requirements. For total sales under $5 million during a 12-month period to the specified class of people above, companies must comply with anti-fraud disclosure rules; for sales of over this amount, companies must disclose additional information, including risk factors, copies of the plans under which the offerings are made, and certain financial statements. These disclosures must be made to all shareholders.

For purposes of this rule, options are considered part of the aggregate sales price, with the option price defined as of the date of grant. In calculating outstanding securities for the 15% rule, all currently exercisable or convertible options, warrants, restricted stock, stock rights, and other securities are counted.

Other exemptions are available for sale to a limited number of accredited or sophisticated investors with appropriate information (these terms are legally defined and generally include officers, directors and/or higher income individuals); small offerings to 35 or fewer non-accredited investors; offerings under $500,000; and offerings only to in-state residents if the offeror does 80% or more of its business and has 80% or more of its assets in-state.

These exemptions from registration are available under federal law. Some states track federal exemptions; some do not. Thirty-nine states have "blue sky laws" (the general name for state securities laws) that comply with the Uniform Securities Act, which is partly based on federal law. Perhaps most important for offerings to employees, however, states that have a specific exemption parallel to the federal Rule 701 exemption (for offerings to employees) are the exception rather than the rule. State registration for such offerings may be needed, therefore, unless other exemptions are met.

Public companies cannot use Rule 701 for an exemption from securities law filings. Instead, most rely on Form S-8, a simplified registration form that can be used to comply with securities laws in conjunction with an offering of options. Public companies do not have to offer a formal prospectus to potential buyers, as closely held companies would. They are, however, required to provide information to employee stock purchasers about the company and its option plan. The S-8 form allows that to be done by reference to already available public documents.

Public companies must also make sure their plan design complies with trading restrictions that apply to corporate insiders. This requires the filing of various reports and the restriction of some trading activity, among other things. These issues are too technical for adequate discussion here. Public companies should consult with their legal counsel on these matters before designing their plan.

MODEL EQUITY COMPENSATION PLAN FOR AN LLC

Brian Hector[1]

Editor's note: This plan is intended solely as a sample of what an equity compensation plan in an LLC looks like. Companies must consult with a qualified attorney to develop a final plan document appropriate to your company as well as applicable state laws. This plan represents one particular approach. There are many possible variations; too many to include in a single model. At appropriate points, however, Corey Rosen of the NCEO has inserted footnote comments to suggest some alternative approaches to specific issues that might be considered; he is solely responsible for the content of those footnotes.

The plan covers options and what we describe in the book as profits interests and capital interests. It does not specifically cover equity appreciation rights. The plan could be adapted to cover these rights by using the language for unit awards for however the company chooses to define these equity appreciation rights. But because their structure is more variable, and their tax consequences potentially more complicated, it is more difficult to have a generic model for these purposes. So while the concepts in this plan could be used for an equity appreciation rights plan, users should work closely with their attorneys to agree on the additional needed material.

[COMPANY] LLC EQUITY COMPENSATION PLAN

The purpose of the [COMPANY] LLC 2009 Equity Compensation Plan (the "Plan") effective as of _____, is to provide (i) designated employees of [COMPANY] LLC, a limited liability company organized under the laws of the State of [_____] (the "Company") and its subsidiaries, (ii) non-employee members of the Board of Managers of

---

1. The footnote material in this article has been prepared by Corey Rosen of the NCEO, who is solely responsible for its content.

the Company (the "Board") with the opportunity to receive grants relating to common units of the Company. The Company believes that the Plan will encourage the participants to contribute to the growth of the Company, thereby benefiting the Company, and will align the economic interests of the participants with those of the owners.

1. Grants

Awards may consist of nonqualified option grants as described below ("Options") and unit awards as described below ("Unit Awards") (collectively referred to herein as "Grants"). All Grants shall be subject to the terms and conditions set forth herein and to such other terms and conditions consistent with this Plan as the Committee deems appropriate and as are specified in writing by the Committee to the individual in a grant instrument or an amendment to the grant instrument (the "Grant Instrument").

2. Units Subject to the Plan

(a) *Units Authorized.* Subject to adjustment as described below, the aggregate number of common units of the Company (the "Units") that may be issued or transferred under the Plan is [_____] Units.

(b) *Determination of Authorized Units.* The Units may be authorized but unissued Units or reacquired Units. If and to the extent Options granted under the Plan terminate, expire, or are canceled, forfeited, exchanged, or surrendered without having been exercised, or if any Unit Awards are forfeited, the Units subject to such Grants shall again be available for purposes of the Plan.

(c) *Adjustments.* If there is any change in the number or kind of Units outstanding by reason of (i) a distribution, spinoff, split of Units, reverse split of Units; recapitalization, or combination or exchange of Units; (ii) a merger, reorganization, or consolidation, (iii) a reclassification; or (iv) any other extraordinary or unusual event affecting the outstanding Units as a class without the Company's receipt of consideration, or if the value of outstanding Units is substantially reduced as a result of a spinoff or the Company's payment of an extraordinary distribution, the maximum number of Units available for Grants, the kind and number of Units covered by outstanding Grants, the kind and number of Units issued and to be issued under the Plan, and the price per Unit or applicable market value of outstanding Grants shall be equitably adjusted by the Committee, to reflect any increase or decrease in the number of, or change in the kind or value of, issued Units to preclude, to the extent practicable, the enlargement or dilution of rights and benefits under the Plan and outstanding Grants; provided, however, that any fractional Units resulting from such adjustment shall be eliminated. Any adjustments to outstanding Grants shall be consistent with Section 409A of the Internal Revenue Code of 1986, as amended and the regulations thereunder (the "Code"), to the extent applicable. Any adjustments determined by the Committee shall be final, binding, and conclusive.

3. Eligibility for Participation

(a) *Eligible Persons.* All employees of the Company ("Employees"), and members of the Board who are not Employees ("Non-Employee Board Members") shall be eligible to participate in the Plan.[2]

(b) *Selection of Grantees.* The Committee shall select the Employees and Non-Employee Board Members ("Grantees") to receive Grants and shall determine the number of Units subject to a particular Grant in such manner as the Committee determines.

4. Options

The Committee may grant Options to an Employee and a Non-Employee Board Member, upon such terms as the Committee deems appropriate, subject to the following provisions:

(a) *Number of Units.* The Committee shall determine the number of Units that will be subject to each Grant of Options to Employees and Non-Employee Board Members.

---

2. The plan could limit those eligible in this section to specific positions, but section (b) allows the plan committee to make decisions about who gets awards at its discretion. This provides a more flexible alternative that allows the company to change who gets awards without changing the plan.

(b) *Type of Option and Price.*[3]

(i) All Options shall be nonqualified options, and not "incentive stock options" under Section 422 of the Code.

(ii) The purchase price (the "Exercise Price") of Units subject to an Option shall be determined by the Committee and shall be equal to or greater than the Market Value (as defined below) of a Unit on the date the Option is granted. The "Fair Market Value" of a Unit shall be, unless the Committee determines otherwise with respect to a particular Grant, as determined by the Committee through any reasonable valuation method authorized under the Code.

(c) *Option Term.* The Committee shall determine the term of each Option.

(d) *Exercisability of Options.*

(i) Options shall become exercisable in accordance with such terms and conditions, consistent with the Plan, as may be determined by the Committee and specified in the Grant Instrument. The Committee may accelerate the exercisability of any or all outstanding Options at any time for any reason.

(ii) The Committee may provide in a Grant Instrument that the Grantee may elect to exercise part or all of an Option before it otherwise has become exercisable. Any Units so purchased shall be restricted Units and shall be subject to a repurchase

---

3. This plan focuses on options and units. Options would be options on either a capital interest or a profits interest. You might want to specify in the plan language that they can be used for either or both. We would suggest you provide that they can be used for either, with the committee having discretion to decide which one for each grant. Note that later in the document, the award of units is discussed. These units could be either a profits interest unit or capital interest unit. However the document is written, the grant agreement should specify whether the option or unit relates to a profits or capital interest. Note also that this plan does not discuss the award of a unit appreciation right, essentially a cash payment for the increase in value of the unit. You could, however, add a new section that would have the same terms and conditions as an option, but would be for a unit appreciation right instead. The language would otherwise be the same as for options.

right in favor of the Company during a specified restriction period, with the repurchase price equal to the lesser of (A) the Exercise Price or (B) the Fair Market Value of such Units at the time of repurchase, or such other restrictions as the Committee deems appropriate.

(e) *Termination of Employment, Disability, or Death.* Except as provided below, an Option may only be exercised while the Grantee is employed by, or providing service to, the Employer (as defined below) as an Employee or Non-Employee Board Member.

(i) If the Grantee ceases to be employed by, or provide service to, the Employer for any reason other than Disability (as defined below), death, or on account of a termination by the Employer for Cause (as defined below), any Option which is otherwise exercisable by the Grantee shall terminate unless exercised within 90 days after the date on which the Grantee ceases to be employed by, or provide service to, the Employer (or within such other period of time as may be specified by the Committee), but in any event no later than the date of expiration of the Option term.[4]

(ii) If the Grantee ceases to be employed by, or provide service to, the Employer on account of a termination by the Employer for Cause, any Option held by the Grantee shall terminate as of the date the Grantee ceases to be employed by, or provide service to, the Employer. In addition, notwithstanding any other provisions of this Section, if the Committee determines that the Grantee has engaged in conduct that constitutes Cause at any time while the Grantee is employed by, or providing service to, the Employer or after the Grantee's termination of employment or service, any Option held by the Grantee shall immediately terminate, and the Grantee shall automatically forfeit all Units underlying any exercised portion of an Option for which the Employer has not yet recorded in its records, upon refund by

---

4.   Nothing would prevent the plan from having a different period than 90 days, although this is the standard practice. A longer period to exercise would be a benefit to the employee but a potential burden to the company.

the Employer of the Exercise Price paid by the Grantee for such Units.

(iii) If the Grantee ceases to be employed by, or provide service to, the Employer because the Grantee is Disabled, any Option which is otherwise exercisable by the Grantee shall terminate unless exercised within [___year/months] after the date on which the Grantee ceases to be employed by, or provide service to, the Employer (or within such other period of time as may be specified by the Committee), but in any event no later than the date of expiration of the Option term. Except as otherwise provided by the Committee, any of the Grantee's Options which are not otherwise exercisable as of the date on which the Grantee ceases to be employed by, or provide service to, the Employer shall terminate as of such date.

(iv) If the Grantee dies while employed by, or providing service to, the Employer or within 90 days after the date on which the Grantee ceases to be employed by, or provide service to, the Employer on account of a termination specified in this Section above (or within such other period of time as may be specified by the Committee), any Option that is otherwise exercisable by the Grantee shall terminate unless exercised within one year after the date on which the Grantee ceases to be employed by, or provide service to, the Employer (or within such other period of time as may be specified by the Committee), but in any event no later than the date of expiration of the Option term. Except as otherwise provided by the Committee, any of the Grantee's Options that are not otherwise exercisable as of the date on which the Grantee ceases to be employed by, or provide service to, the Employer shall terminate as of such date.

(v) Definitions:

(A) "Employer" shall mean the Company and its subsidiaries.

(B) "Employed by, or provide service to, the Employer" shall mean employment or service as an Employee or Non-Employee Board Member (so that, for purposes of exercising Options and satisfying conditions with respect to Unit

Awards, a Grantee shall not be considered to have terminated employment or service until the Grantee ceases to be
an Employee and Non-Employee Board Member), unless
the Committee determines otherwise.

(C) "Disability" shall mean a Grantee's becoming disabled
within the meaning of Section 22(e)(3) of the Code, or as
otherwise determined by the Committee.

(D) "Cause" shall mean, except to the extent specified otherwise by the Committee, a finding by the Committee that
the Grantee has engaged in fraud, embezzlement, theft,
commission of a felony, or proven dishonesty.[5]

(f) *Exercise of Options.* Options may be exercisable, in whole or in part,
by delivering a notice of exercise to the Company with payment of
the Exercise Price. The Grantee shall pay the Exercise Price for an
Option in cash, with the approval of the Committee, by delivering
Units owned by the Grantee (including Units acquired in connection
with the exercise of an Option, subject to such restrictions as the
Committee deems appropriate) and having a Fair Market Value on
the date of exercise equal to the Exercise Price or by attestation (on
a form prescribed by the Committee) to ownership of Units having a
Fair Market Value on the date of exercise equal to the Exercise Price,
or by such other method as the Committee may approve. The Grantee
shall pay the Exercise Price and the amount of any withholding tax
due (pursuant to Section 6) at the time of exercise.

5. Unit Awards

The Committee may issue or transfer Units to an Employee or Non-
Employee Board Members, upon such terms as the Committee deems
appropriate.

(a) *General.* Units issued or transferred pursuant to Unit Awards may
be issued or transferred for consideration or for no consideration,
may be subject to restrictions or no restrictions, as determined by

---

5. The term "Cause" is a very fact-specific phrase that can be broadened or limited
    as the case may be, depending on the individual circumstances of the LLC.

the Committee and may be structured as capital interests or profits interests in the Company for tax purposes. The period of time during which the Unit Awards will remain subject to restrictions will be designated in the Grant Instrument as the "Restriction Period."

(b) *Number of Units.* The Committee shall determine the number of Units to be issued or transferred pursuant to a Unit Award and the restrictions applicable to such Units.

(c) *Requirement of Employment or Service.* If the Grantee ceases to be employed by, or provide service to, the Employer during a period designated in the Grant Instrument as the Restriction Period, or if other specified conditions are not met, the Unit Award shall terminate as to all Units covered by the Unit Award as to which the restrictions have not lapsed, and those Units must be immediately returned to the Employer. The Committee may, however, provide for complete or partial exceptions to this requirement as it deems appropriate.

(d) *Restrictions on Transfer.* During the Restriction Period, a Grantee may not sell, assign, transfer, pledge, or otherwise dispose of the Unit Awards except to a successor pursuant to Section 7.

(e) *Right to Vote and Receive Distributions.* Unless the Committee determines otherwise, during the Restriction Period, a Grantee shall have the right to vote Units subject to Unit Awards and to receive any distributions paid on such Units, subject to any restrictions deemed appropriate by the Committee, including, without limitation, the achievement of specific performance goals.

(f) *Lapse of Restrictions.* All restrictions imposed on Unit Awards shall lapse upon the expiration of the applicable Restriction Period and the satisfaction of all conditions imposed by the Committee. The Committee may determine, as to any or all Unit Awards, that the restrictions shall lapse without regard to any Restriction Period.

(g) *Treatment as a Member of the Company.* Each Grantee who is granted a Unit Award intended to be a profits interest and who has timely made an election under Section 83(b) of the Code with respect to such Unit Award shall be treated as a Member of the Company for all federal, state, and local tax purposes.

6. Withholding of Taxes

(a) *Required Withholding.* All Grants under the Plan shall be subject to applicable federal (including FICA), state and local tax withholding requirements. The Employer may require that the Grantee or other person receiving or exercising Grants pay to the Employer the amount of any federal, state, or local taxes that the Employer is required to withhold with respect to such Grants, or the Employer may deduct from other wages paid by the Employer the amount of any withholding taxes due with respect to such Grants.

(b) *Election to Withhold Units.* If the Committee so permits, a Grantee may elect to satisfy the Employer's income tax withholding obligation with respect to a Grant by having Units withheld up to an amount that does not exceed the Grantee's minimum applicable withholding tax rate for federal (including FICA), state, and local tax liabilities. The election must be in a form and manner prescribed by the Committee and may be subject to the prior approval of the Committee.

7. Transferability of Grants

(a) *Nontransferability of Grants.* Except as provided below, only the Grantee may exercise rights under a Grant during the Grantee's lifetime. A Grantee may not transfer those rights except (i) by will or by the laws of descent and distribution or (ii) if permitted in any specific case by the Committee, pursuant to a domestic relations order or otherwise as permitted by the Committee. When a Grantee dies, the personal representative or other person entitled to succeed to the rights of the Grantee may exercise such rights. Any such successor must furnish proof satisfactory to the Company of his or her right to receive the Grant under the Grantee's will or under the applicable laws of descent and distribution.

(b) *Transfer of Options.* Notwithstanding the foregoing, the Committee may provide, in a Grant Instrument, that a Grantee may transfer Options to family members, or one or more trusts or other entities for the benefit of or owned by family members, consistent with the applicable securities laws, according to such terms as the Committee may determine; provided that the Grantee receives no consideration for the transfer of an Option and the transferred Option shall continue to be subject to the same terms and conditions as were applicable to the Option immediately before the transfer.

8. Right of First Refusal; Repurchase Right

(a) *Offer.* At any time an individual desires to sell, encumber, or otherwise dispose of Units that were distributed to him or her under this Plan and that are transferable, the individual may do so only pursuant to a bona fide written offer, and the individual shall first offer the Units to the Company by giving the Company written notice disclosing: (i) the name of the proposed transferee of the Units; (ii) the number of Units proposed to be transferred or encumbered; (iii) the proposed price; (iv) all other terms of the proposed transfer; and (v) a written copy of the proposed offer. Within 60 days after receipt of such notice, the Company shall have the option to purchase all or part of such Units at the price and on the terms described in the written notice, provided that the Company may pay such price in installments over a period not to exceed four years, at the discretion of the Committee.

(b) *Sale.* If the Company does not exercise the option to purchase Units, as provided above, the individual shall have the right to sell, encumber, or otherwise dispose of the Units described in subsection (a) at the price and on the terms of the transfer set forth in the written notice to the Company, provided such transfer is effected within 30 days after the expiration of the option period. If the transfer is not effected within such period, the Company must again be given an option to purchase, as provided above.

(c) *Purchase by the Company.* If a Grantee ceases to be employed by, or provide service to, the Employer, the Company shall have the right to purchase all or part of any Unit distributed to him or her under this Plan at its then current Fair Market Value (or at such other price as may be established in the Grant Instrument); provided, however, that such repurchase shall be made in accordance with applicable law and shall be made in accordance with applicable accounting rules to avoid adverse accounting treatment.

(d) *Operating Agreement.* Notwithstanding the provisions of this Section, if the Operating Agreement provides a right of first refusal or repurchase rights with respect to Units, the provisions of this Section shall not apply to the extent inconsistent with the Operating Agreement, unless the Committee determines otherwise.

9. Change of Control of the Company

(a) *Definition of Change of Control.* As used herein, a "Change of Control" shall be deemed to have occurred if:

(i) Any "person" (as such term is used in sections 13(d) and 14(d) of the Securities Exchange Act of 1934 (the "Exchange Act")) becomes a "beneficial owner" (as defined in Rule 13d-3 under the Exchange Act), directly or indirectly, of equity securities in the Company representing more than 50% of the voting power of the then outstanding equity securities of the Company; provided that a Change of Control shall not be deemed to occur as a result of a transaction in which the Company becomes a subsidiary of another company and in which the owners of the Company, immediately prior to the transaction, will beneficially own, immediately after the transaction, equity securities entitling such owners to more than 50% of all votes to which all owners of the parent company would be entitled in the election of members; or

(ii) The consummation of (A) a merger or consolidation of the Company with another company where the owners of the Company, immediately prior to the merger or consolidation, will not beneficially own, immediately after the merger or consolidation, equity securities entitling such members to more than 50% of all votes to which all owners of the surviving company would be entitled in the election of members, (B) a sale or other disposition of all or substantially all of the assets of the Company, or (C) a liquidation or dissolution of the Company.

(b) *Acceleration.* Upon a Change of Control, unless the Committee determines otherwise, (i) all outstanding Options shall automatically accelerate and become fully exercisable and (ii) all outstanding Unit

Awards shall become fully vested and the restrictions and conditions on all outstanding Unit Awards shall immediately lapse.[6]

10. Requirements for Issuance or Transfer of Units

(a) *Operating Agreement.* It shall be a condition precedent to the receipt of Units under the Plan that a Grantee execute the Company's Operating Agreement, as in effect from time to time, with respect to any Units issued or distributed pursuant to the Plan.

(b) *Limitations on Issuance or Transfer of Units.* No Units shall be issued or transferred in connection with any Grant hereunder unless and until all legal requirements applicable to the issuance or transfer of such Units have been complied with to the satisfaction of the Committee, including all requirements of the Company's Operating Agreement. The Committee shall have the right to condition any Grant made to any Grantee hereunder on such Grantee's undertaking in writing to comply with such restrictions on his or her subsequent disposition of such Units as the Committee shall deem necessary or advisable.

11. Miscellaneous

(a) *Amendment and Termination of the Plan.* The Committee may amend or terminate the Plan at any time. The Plan shall terminate on the day immediately preceding the tenth anniversary of its effective date, unless the Plan is terminated earlier by the Committee or is extended

---

6. Some companies do not normally provide for acceleration upon a change in control. The argument is that an acquirer, especially of a company whose value is primarily the intellectual capital of those who work for it, will be reluctant to see awards fully vest on a change of control because the employees could have enough money to leave. In these cases, the acquirer may pay less for the company because of these rights. Alternatively, the company might agree that the awards would vest only after the employee has worked for the acquiring company for some period of time. The potential problem here, of course, is that employees might find such a provision demotivating while they are still employed by the LLC. The language here does provide the committee discretion to provide for an arrangement other than full vesting, so the language should be made more restrictive only if the company is absolutely certain it does not want to fully vest awards on acquisition.

by the Committee. A termination or amendment of the Plan that occurs after a Grant is made shall not materially impair the rights of a Grantee unless the Grantee consents or unless the Committee acts under the Plan. The termination of the Plan shall not impair the power and authority of the Committee with respect to an outstanding Grant. Whether or not the Plan has terminated, an outstanding Grant may be terminated or amended under the Plan or may be amended by agreement of the Company and the Grantee consistent with the Plan.

(b) *Grants in Connection with Company Transactions and Otherwise.* Nothing contained in this Plan shall be construed to (i) limit the right of the Committee to make Grants under this Plan in connection with the acquisition, by purchase, lease, merger, consolidation, or otherwise, of the business or assets of any company, firm or association, including Grants to employees thereof who become employees of the Company, or for other proper company purposes, or (ii) limit the right of the Company to make other awards outside of this Plan. Without limiting the foregoing, the Committee may make a Grant to an employee of another company who becomes an employee by reason of a merger, consolidation, acquisition of securities or property, reorganization, or liquidation involving the Company or any of its subsidiaries in substitution for a grant made by such company. The terms and conditions of the substitute grants may vary from the terms and conditions required by the Plan and from those of the substituted incentives. The Committee shall prescribe the provisions of the substitute grants.

(c) *Funding.* This Plan shall be unfunded. The Company shall not be required to establish any special or separate fund or to make any other segregation of assets to assure the payment of any Grants under this Plan. In no event shall interest be paid or accrued on any Grant, including unpaid installments of Grants.

(d) *Compliance with Law.* The Plan, the exercise of Options and the obligations of the Company to issue or transfer Units shall be subject to all applicable laws and to approvals by any governmental or regulatory agency as may be required. It is the intent of the Company that, to the extent applicable, Grants made under the Plan comply with the requirements of Section 409A of the Code and the regulations thereunder. To the extent that any legal requirement as set forth in the Plan ceases to be required under applicable law, the Committee may determine that such Plan provision shall cease to apply. The Committee may revoke any Grant if it is contrary to law or modify a Grant or the Plan to bring a Grant or the Plan into compliance with any applicable law or regulation. The Committee may, in its sole discretion, agree to limit its authority under this Section.

(e) *Administration.* The Plan shall be administered and interpreted by the Committee consisting of members of the Board, and which shall be appointed by the Board. Unless otherwise restricted by the Board, the Committee shall have the sole authority to determine the individuals to whom grants shall be made, the size and terms of the grants, and the time when the grants will be made and the duration of any applicable exercise or restriction period.

(f) *Governing Law.* The validity, construction, interpretation, and effect of the Plan and Grant Instruments issued under the Plan shall be governed and construed by and determined in accordance with the laws of the State of [_____], without giving effect to the conflict of laws provisions thereof.

This plan document is included in Microsoft Word format and (for those who cannot open the Word document) Rich Text Format on the CD-ROM bound into the back of this book.

ABOUT THE AUTHORS

Brian Hector is a partner with Morgan, Lewis & Bockius LLP in Chicago and co-chair of the firm's national ESOP practice. He is a frequent contributor to NCEO publications and speaker at NCEO meetings on equity compensation and ESOPs. Mr. Hector designs all types of executive compensation arrangements that are both equity and non-equity benefits, including stock options, deferred compensation plans, long-term incentive plans, SARs, and phantom stock plans.

Daniel N. Janich is the managing principal of Janich Law Group. He has extensive experience counseling businesses and executives on all aspects of employee benefits and executive compensation, including tax, securities law, and ERISA. He also litigates employee benefits and executive compensation claims. A former chair of the Chicago Bar Association's Employee Benefits Committee, Mr. Janich is currently associate senior editor of *Employee Benefits Law* and management co-chair of the Reporting and Disclosure Subcommittee of the ABA Labor and Employment Law Section's Employee Benefits Committee. He is also a Fellow of the American College of Employee Benefits Counsel. Mr. Janich received a B.A. degree cum laude in history from Marian College, Indianapolis; a J.D. degree from The John Marshall Law School, Chicago; and an LL.M. in Taxation degree from DePaul University, Chicago.

Alan A. Nadel serves as the managing director of Strategic Apex Group LLC, a compensation consulting firm with offices in New York, London, and Los Angeles. He has more than 38 years of experience serving a diverse range of clients, advising on matters relating to governance, executive and board of directors compensation, employee benefits, retirement programs, and income and estate planning. In his current practice, Alan advises boards of directors about the design and implementation of executive and director programs, including the strategic, financial, funding, accounting, and tax considerations, as well as various aspects of corporate governance. Also, he has represented various companies and senior executives in negotiations concerning employment agreements, severance programs, and change-in-control arrangements. Alan also has provided expert testimony in both civil and criminal matters. Clients include public and private companies, domestic as well as international. Before establishing his company, Alan was a partner in two major accounting firms, including Arthur Andersen, where he established the compensation consulting practice and served as Managing Partner – Human Capital. Alan started his career with the Internal Revenue Service. Alan is the author of *Accounting for Equity Compensation* (1st and 2nd editions) and is a coauthor of *The Employee Benefits Handbook*. He has lectured at various law schools and business schools and is a frequent speaker before professional and industry groups.

Corey Rosen is the NCEO's executive director. He cofounded the NCEO in 1981 after working for five years as a professional staff member in the U.S. Senate, where he helped draft legislation on employee ownership plans. Before that, he taught political science at Ripon College. He is the author or coauthor of many books and over 100 articles on employee ownership, and coauthor (with John Case and Martin Staubus) of *Equity: Why Employee Ownership Is Good for Business* (Harvard Business School Press, 2005). He was the subject of an extensive interview in *Inc.* magazine in August 2000; has appeared frequently on CNN, PBS, NPR, and other network programs; and is regularly quoted in the *Wall Street Journal,* the *New York Times,* and other leading publications. He has a Ph.D. in political science from Cornell University and serves on the advisory board of the Certified Equity Professional Institute. He also served on the board of directors of the Great Place to Work Institute, creator of *Fortune* magazine's "100 Best Companies to Work for in America" list.

ABOUT THE NCEO

The National Center for Employee Ownership (NCEO) is widely considered to be the leading authority in employee ownership in the U.S. and the world. Established in 1981 as a nonprofit information and membership organization, it now has over 2,500 members, including companies, professionals, unions, government officials, academics, and interested individuals. It is funded entirely through the work it does.

The NCEO's mission is to provide the most objective, reliable information possible about employee ownership at the most affordable price possible. As part of the NCEO's commitment to providing objective information, it does not lobby or provide ongoing consulting services. The NCEO publishes a variety of materials on employee ownership and participation, holds dozens of seminars, conference calls, Webinars, and conferences on employee ownership annually, and offers a variety of online courses. The NCEO's work includes extensive contacts with the media, both through articles written for trade and professional publications and through interviews with reporters. It has written or edited several books for outside publishers. The NCEO maintains an extensive Web site at www.nceo.org.

See the following page for information on membership benefits and fees. To join, see the order form at the end of this section, visit our Web site at www.nceo.org, or telephone us at 510-208-1300.

Membership Benefits

NCEO members receive the following benefits:

- The bimonthly newsletter *Employee Ownership Report,* which covers ESOPs, equity compensation, and employee participation.
- Access to the members-only area of the NCEO's Web site, which includes a searchable newsletter archive, a discussion forum, a database of service providers, and more.

- Substantial discounts on publications, online courses, and events produced by the NCEO.

- Free access to live Webinars and conference calls.

- The right to contact the NCEO for answers to general or specific questions regarding employee ownership.

An introductory NCEO membership costs $90 for one year ($100 outside the U.S.) and covers an entire company at all locations, a single professional offering services in this field, or a single individual with a business interest in employee ownership. Full-time students and faculty members who are not employed in the business sector may join at the academic rate of $40 for one year ($50 outside the U.S.).

Selected NCEO Publications

The NCEO offers a variety of publications on all aspects of employee ownership and participation. Below are some of our publications.

We publish new books and revise old ones on a yearly basis. To obtain the most current information on what we have available, visit us on the Web at www.nceo.org or call us at 510-208-1300.

Equity Compensation

- This book, *Equity Compensation for Limited Liability Companies,* describes how equity compensation works in an LLC and provides a model plan document.

    $25 for NCEO members, $35 for nonmembers

- *The Stock Options Book* is a straightforward, comprehensive overview covering the legal, accounting, regulatory, and design issues involved in implementing a stock option or stock purchase plan.

    $25 for NCEO members, $35 for nonmembers

- *The Decision-Maker's Guide to Equity Compensation* describes the various types of equity compensation, how they work, and how to decide how much to give and to whom.

    $35 for NCEO members, $50 for nonmembers

- *Beyond Stock Options* is a complete guide, including annotated model plans, to phantom stock, restricted stock, stock appreciation rights, performance awards, and more. Includes a CD with plan documents.

  $35 for NCEO members, $50 for nonmembers

- *Accounting for Equity Compensation* is a guide to the accounting rules that govern equity compensation programs in the U.S.

  $25 for NCEO members, $35 for nonmembers

Employee Stock Ownership Plans (ESOPs)

- *Understanding ESOPs* is an overview of the issues involved in establishing and operating an ESOP.

  $25 for NCEO members, $35 for nonmembers

- *Selling to an ESOP* is a guide for owners, managers, and advisors of closely held businesses, with a particular focus on the tax-deferred Section 1042 "rollover" for C corporation owners.

  $25 for NCEO members, $35 for nonmembers

- *S Corporation ESOPs* introduces the reader to how ESOPs work and then discusses the legal, valuation, administrative, and other issues associated with S corporation ESOPs.

  $25 for NCEO members, $35 for nonmembers

Other

- *The Journal of Employee Ownership Law and Finance* is the only professional journal solely devoted to employee ownership. Articles cover ESOPs, equity compensation, and related subjects in depth.

  One-year subscription (four issues):
  $75 for NCEO members, $100 for nonmembers

To join the NCEO as a member or to order publications, use the order form on the following page, order online at www.nceo.org, or call us at 510-208-1300. If you join at the same time you order publications, you will receive the members-only publication discounts.

Order Form

This book is published by the National Center for Employee Ownership (NCEO). You can order additional copies online at our Web site, www.nceo.org; by telephoning the NCEO at 510-208-1300; by faxing this page to the NCEO at 510-272-9510; or by sending this page to the NCEO at 1736 Franklin Street, 8th Floor, Oakland, CA 94612. If you join as an NCEO member with this order, or are already an NCEO member, you will pay the discounted member price for any publications you order.

Name

Organization

Address

City, State, Zip (Country)

Telephone   Fax   Email

Method of Payment: ❑ Check (payable to "NCEO")   ❑ Visa   ❑ M/C   ❑ AMEX

Credit Card Number

Signature   Exp. Date

Checks are accepted only for orders from the U.S. and must be in U.S. currency.

Title	Qty.	Price	Total

Subtotal	$
Sales Tax	$
Shipping	$
Membership	$
TOTAL DUE	$

Tax: California residents add 9.75% sales tax (on publications only, not membership or Journal subscriptions)

Shipping: In the U.S., first publication $5, each add'l $1; elsewhere, we charge exact shipping costs to your credit card, plus a $10 handling surcharge; no shipping charges for membership

Introductory NCEO Membership: $90 for one year ($100 outside the U.S.)